The Complete Guide to

Leopard Gecko Care and Ownership

Samantha Slevens

LP Media Inc. Publishing
Text copyright © 2023 by LP Media Inc.
All rights reserved.
No part of this book may be reproduced or transmitted in any form or by any means, electronic or mechanical, including photocopying, recording, or by an information storage and retrieval system – except by a reviewer who may quote brief passages in a review to be printed in a magazine or newspaper – without permission in writing from the publisher. For information address LP Media Inc. Publishing, 1405 Kingsview Ln N, Plymouth, MN 55447
www.lpmedia.org

Publication Data

Samantha Slevens
The Complete Guide to Leopard Gecko Care and Ownership – First edition.
Summary: "Successfully caring for and owning a Leopard Gecko"
Provided by publisher.
ISBN: 978-1-954288-95-9
[1. The Complete Guide to Leopard Gecko Care and Ownership – Non-Fiction] I. Title.

This book has been written with the published intent to provide accurate and authoritative information in regard to the subject matter included. While every reasonable precaution has been taken in preparation of this book the author and publisher expressly disclaim responsibility for any errors, omissions, or adverse effects arising from the use or application of the information contained inside. The techniques and suggestions are to be used at the reader's discretion and are not to be considered a substitute for professional veterinary care. If you suspect a medical problem with your Leopard Gecko, consult your veterinarian.

Design by Sorin Rădulescu
First paperback edition, 2023

TABLE OF CONTENTS

Chapter 1
Why Choose a Leopard Gecko? 1
A Great Starter Lizard 3
Especially Good for Kids 5
The History of Leopard Geckos 7
Leos in the Wild 8
Domesticated Leopard Geckos 9

Chapter 2
Where to Get Your Leopard Gecko 11
Pet Store vs. Breeders 11
Big Chain Pet Stores 13
Exotic Pet Stores 15
Breeders 16
Lizard & Reptile Shows 20

Chapter 3
Choosing Your Perfect Leopard Gecko 23
Choose a Healthy-Looking Gecko 23
Choose a Gecko Showing Normal, Healthy Behavior 26
What Sex, Size, Number, and Age to Choose? 27

Chapter 4
Leopard Gecko Morphs 31
Introduction to Morphs.. 31
Terminology Associated with Morphs.......................... 34
The Most Common Leopard Gecko Morphs 37
Rarity and Pricing.. 43

Chapter 5
The Perfect Vivarium 45
Welcoming Your Leopard Gecko Home........................ 45
Vivarium Options 47
Where to Put the Tank 53
How to Clean Your Tank.. 55

Chapter 6
Substrate, Hides, and Decorations 61
Substrate.. 61
Plants.. 63
Hides... 64
Decorations or Tank Decor... 66
Cleaning Substrate and Decor 68

Chapter 7
Lighting and Humidity 71
Leopard Gecko Heating Needs 71
Thermometer 73

Heat and Lighting Choices 75
Humidity 76

Chapter 8
Food and Water 79
Food 79
Supplements 86
Water 87

Chapter 9
Health and Wellness 91
Be Vigilant 92
Keep Them Active 96
Recognizing Health Problems 97
Most Common Ailments 98
Shedding and Tail Dropping 103

Chapter 10
Handling Tips 107
All Geckos Are Different 107
Build Trust and Take It Slow 109
Picking Up Your Leo 109
Advanced Tips 112
Kids 116

Chapter 11
Breeding 121
Choosing to Breed 122
Breeding 123
Determining Sex 127
Special Care for Females 127
Egg Laying 128
Incubation 129
Hatching 132
Hatchlings 133

Chapter 12
Other Geckos 137
Other Geckos and Reptilian Pets 137

CHAPTER 1

Why Choose a Leopard Gecko?

The Leopard Gecko (*Eublepharis macularius*) is a ground-dwelling lizard with origins in the dry areas of Iran, Afghanistan, Pakistan, Nepal, and India. In addition to their common and scientific names, these smiling reptiles are also known as Desert Fat-tailed Geckos, Spotted Fat-tailed Geckos, Fat-tailed Geckos, and Panther Geckos.

Their natural color is an attractive yellowish-brown with dark spots all over the body. This coloration is ideal camouflage in their natural habitat. However, the pet trade and captive breeding have now produced over

■ *natural habitat of Leopard Geckos*

Chapter 1: Why Choose a Leopard Gecko?

one hundred – and counting! – awesome color variations and morphs, including geckos that no longer have characteristic spots. Sometimes these morphs were deliberately created by breeders. Others have been colorful genetic accidents.

We now have bright yellow or orange, albino, pale pastel hues, spotted, plain, and striped leopard geckos, and they are all lovely. Twenty-seven morphs are particularly popular and are used as the base for new morphs. The rarer ones could set you back a few thousand dollars. Unlike chameleons, geckos do not change color except when they shed and may look a little pale. However, after the shed, they will eventually become more vibrant.

Thanks to a range of appealing features and the fact that they are hardy, these characterful little geckos are now popular pets all over the world. But what makes them such fantastic pets, especially for a beginner reptile owner?

A Great Starter Lizard

> *Leopard geckos make great entry-level lizards for first-time reptile owners. They stay small, so they don't require an enormous enclosure (a 20-gallon tank is perfect); they're nocturnal, so they don't require a bunch of extra specialty (UVB) lighting; and almost every leopard gecko that I've encountered has had a sweet and docile disposition.*
>
> PATRICK KAMBEROS
> *Cold Blooded and Bizarre*

Leopard geckos are fantastic pets for anyone interested in exploring the world of reptiles. They are beautiful little lizards with thick, soft tails; textured but smooth scales; and permanent, heart-melting smiles. They are also a relatively small species, growing only 7 to 10 inches and living long enough to be a part of the family, like a dog. They weigh 40 to 100 grams. The males are larger and weigh more than the females.

The average lifespan of a leopard gecko in the wild is three to eight years, as they face several predators. Females have shorter lives because of the demands of egg-laying. Though leopard geckos have a life span of 10 to 20 years in captivity, the oldest known gecko was 32 years old. For this reason, it's a good idea to have a '10-year plan' when purchasing a pet to ensure your gecko can stay with you even if you need to move while it is in your care.

Sometimes reptilian pets can be difficult companions to care for because of their very specific needs when it comes to habitat, environmental conditions, and food. This is not the case with leopards, however, as they are easy to handle, and their care requirements are considerably lower and less demanding than those of other reptile species. In addition, adult geckos only need to be fed every two to three days. Juveniles and babies can be a bit higher maintenance, as they need feeding more frequently.

Another advantage is that, unlike some other pets, these lizards do not smell (if you keep their tank or terrarium clean). This is due to the fact that they only eat insects, and their fecal matter is dry and granular. This means you can keep the tank in your bedroom or even a living room without an odor issue. Feeder insect colonies do smell, so they should not be in a space where people spend a lot of time!

Some reptiles can be challenging or less engaging as pets because of their sleeping schedules, but leopard geckos are perfect! Captive geckos are primarily nocturnal, so they tend to be most active when you are home from school or work. Once accustomed to you and being handled, these great companions are friendly and sociable and love to spend time with you and go exploring when possible.

I used to set my leopard gecko up in a bin with a towel and have him near me while I did my homework after school. Once homework was done, I would get him snuggled up in a blanket or towel, and we would sit on the couch and watch television together. His favorite movie was *Godzilla*. No, seriously!

As stated, these creatures are very popular pets thanks to a range of factors. As a result, there are tons of great products and resources available to owners. However, it can sometimes be difficult to find the best – accurate and practical – information about leopard geckos. This guide will give you all the information necessary to successfully adopt and care for your new scaley family member.

Photo Courtesy of Chelsea O'Brien

Especially Good for Kids

> *Leopard geckos make a great first-time pet in general. They are low maintenance and don't need attention every day like other species of reptiles or pets in general. This makes them ideal for anyone who doesn't have much time on their hands. They don't require much space either! My first pet was, ironically, a leopard gecko when I was around seven, and I loved it. Throughout my life, I've always had at least one!*
>
> SEAN BERGMAN
> *E-ville Geckos*

Leopard geckos are relatively hardy, and the adults can handle the boisterous love of children who may be a little rougher than they mean to be. They can also fit perfectly in a child's bedroom or common area, as they do not require a massive enclosure.

These geckos can be a bit more temperamental as babies. This is natural, as they are at the highest risk of predation when they are young and vulnerable. Sometimes they feel the need to protect themselves from us. As a result, it is vitally important to build a trusting relationship with your gecko and have patience as it gets used to human handling. Purchasing your gecko from a reputable breeder or small exotic pet store is often better as the geckos are handled more often than those from larger chain stores and can come to you with some experience of interacting with humans.

These little guys are often "all bark and no bite," but even if they try, their bite is harmless as their teeth are often too small to puncture the thick skin on human hands. However, because their jaws are strong relative to their size, a bite can feel like a hard pinch. On the extremely rare occasion that one of the little teeth punctures the skin, you need to disinfect it properly. Their usually sweet nature makes them an unaggressive pet and probably one of the most docile reptile you can get. Once these geckos are trusting, they are happy being held by children of all ages and enjoy walking across trusted hands.

Although they are not aggressive by nature, they must – like all living creatures – be treated with respect to establish and maintain their trust. If they feel threatened, cornered, or are territorial of their enclosure, they may react by giving a little chomp. However, due to their timid nature, they are typically far more likely to run off rather than stand their ground and fight or attack. This is because these reptiles are prey to various animals living in their natural habitat, and captive geckos retain their "wild" self-preservation instincts. So, when it comes to "fight or flight," they usually choose flight because, in the wild, that gives them their greatest chance of survival.

When cared for properly and handled correctly, these geckos will enjoy being handled and can even learn to eat from your hand.

Photo Courtesy of Maggie Hyatt
Owner Aaron Wilson

Photo Courtesy of Dean Host Jr. Origami Geckos

The History of Leopard Geckos

Most leopard geckos available in the pet trade were originally collected in Pakistan. These reptiles breed so easily in captivity that most leopard geckos sold today are not wild-caught but captive-bred. Your pet is unlikely to have ever known any life other than one in a tank.

These lizards do not enjoy too much moisture as the climate in their natural habitat is dry and arid. Leos live in areas with rocky crags and dry grasslands and are not a desert species, so there are no sand dunes or cacti where they are from. They prefer the cover of rocks and scrub brush so that they can hide from aerial predators like birds and sneak up on insects for a quick snack.

Their history in the pet trade is quite extensive, as they were the first widely domesticated lizard species. They found their way into the pet market in the 1960s but became more popular in the 1970s. Leopard geckos gained popularity as pets in the United States, specifically in the 1980s and 1990s. That's over 50 years of domesticated breeding. No wonder they are such popular, established pets and one of the most kept lizards today!

Leos in the Wild

Wild leopard geckos are typically most active during dawn and dusk. The term for this is crepuscular rather than nocturnal or diurnal.

This behavioral pattern is incredibly important because it allows them to avoid the scorching temperatures of the wild areas they live in, where the temperatures can reach over 150°F! This would be death for most creatures. At dawn and dusk, temperatures are not too high, and geckos have an ideal window to search for their meals.

Their life in the wild is certainly challenging, and while their life span in the wild is thought to be up to 8 years, they must evade several predators to survive this long. A gecko is a desirable snack or meal for larger reptiles, snakes, and foxes. Apart from hunting at times when they are least likely to run into a predator, leopard geckos also have a few other features that help them avoid predation.

FUN FACT
They Can Blink

Leopard geckos are unique among lizards—they are one of only a few lizards with moveable eyelids. These noteworthy crinkled eyelids give leopard geckos a sweet and expressive countenance beloved by many. Most geckos have a singular transparent, immovable eyelid they keep clean by licking. In contrast, the leopard gecko's fully moveable eyelids allow it to close its eyes to better protect them from injury.

These little reptiles have very sharp hearing, a keen sense of smell, and excellent sight, and as mentioned, geckos have ideal coloring and markings to blend into the rocks and plants around them. They can also take cover in holes and cracks between rocks where they are out of reach. Finally, while they are not vocal, they can produce surprisingly loud barks and squeaks when they are threatened and stressed.

Domesticated Leopard Geckos

Domesticated leopard geckos have a significant advantage over their wild brethren. There are many resources that we pet owners provide to them daily that they would otherwise have to travel large distances and spend a lot of time finding.

These searches for resources leave wild leopard geckos open to predation. Having food and water easily accessible increases the life span of captive geckos. Pet leopard geckos can live for 20 years, and the oldest one is believed to be 32!

By providing clean water, regular feeding schedules, regulated temperatures, medical care, and mental stimulation, leopard geckos are offered everything they need to live long and happy lives. There are also no predators (if your other pets, like dogs and cats, do not get too curious) in captivity.

At-a-Glance Fact Sheet

- Leopard geckos are the most popular pet lizards in the pet industry.
- They are also known as Desert Fat-tailed Geckos, Spotted Fat-tailed Geckos, Fat-tailed Geckos, and Panther Geckos.
- Their origins are the dry areas of Iran, Afghanistan, Pakistan, Nepal, and India
- They're great for kids as they have a relaxed temperament.
- They do not have exacting requirements in terms of habitat.
- They do not require massive enclosures and only feed a few times a week.
- They stay small and reach a maximum length of 7-10 inches.
- They have a lifespan of 10 to 20 years in captivity but can live even longer with the correct care.
- They come in a dazzling variety of colors and patterns.
- They face a range of predators in the wild and can be skittish until they get used to human handling.

CHAPTER 2

Where to Get Your Leopard Gecko

The first major decision you need to make is where you are going to get your new family member. You could go to a pet store, a breeder, one of the large chain pet stores, or exotic pet stores.

There are pros and cons for each that you need to consider *before* you head off to purchase your leopard gecko. For example, geckos in the wild can contract diseases from each other that spread like wildfire. These diseases are not present in a domestic atmosphere if reptiles are purchased from a reputable source.

Pet Store vs. Breeders

> *When choosing your leopard gecko, it's always best to find a reputable breeder that offers quality geckos. When buying from a reputable breeder, not only are you supporting small business owners, but you will also know exactly what morph your gecko is as well as what sex. Most often, when buying from a pet store, the sex and morph are unknown.*
>
> **MIKE RICHARD**
> *Maritime Geckos*

Chapter 2: Where to Get Your Leopard Gecko

Leopard geckos are such common pets now that they are often available at chain pet stores. However, often these geckos are not well handled, and they may also not be sourced in the best way. The chains may pursue the cheapest option. On the other hand, small pet stores are usually a better choice for picking a gecko that is used to humans and has been responsibly acquired.

In addition, buying a gecko at a pet store can be very helpful because employees there can guide you in choosing the correct equipment for a reptile enclosure. It is always important to do research before buying supplies. It can also be helpful to have your enclosure and heat system purchased in advance, so you know the tank is at an adequate temperature before placing your new gecko inside it.

Also, be sure to do some research and check reviews of the pet store you have chosen and use your best judgment in determining if the animals are in good health. How to determine a gecko's health by looking at it will be discussed in later chapters. Sometimes in large chains, animals get ill from transportation or are carrying diseases from the facility they were previously at. Purchasing directly from a breeder can usually remove these unknowns.

Big Chain Pet Stores

> *Most pet stores purchase their animals from a mass breeder at a low cost and are not completely versed in the proper care of those animals. In my personal experience with pet stores, the leopard geckos always look too skinny and sickly, and, generally, there's just not enough customer interaction and education.*
>
> STEPHANIE DILLON
> *Granite State Geckos*

Massive, franchised pet stores are local and convenient, but they do not always source their reptiles reputably. Some of them purchase the cheapest bulk option for resale. Places that sell reptiles in bulk like this are called reptile mills. The purpose of these facilities is to crank out as many reptiles as inexpensively as possible, to sell as quickly as they can. The condition of some of these facilities can be overcrowded and may lead to health issues among the animals.

An undercover PETA investigator describes the horrifying scene at these locations, stating that there were "tens of thousands of [reptiles] confined to barren, filthy, crowded plastic tubs and deprived of even the most basic necessities."[1] In addition, severely injured and ill animals may be left to suffer for days until they are killed in a slow and painful manner and disposed of.

Having a huge number of animals at any location means they do not get the individualized attention they need. Animals that come from reptile mills have a much higher risk of carrying diseases due to the number of animals present, and therefore, your pet may have a shorter life span,

---

1 "Reptiles Suffer, Left to Die at Another Massive PetSmart Supplier Mill," PETA Exposés and Undercover Investigations, April 6, 2022, https://investigations.peta.org/reptiles-suffer-petsmart/.

even if you do everything right. Also, if you unknowingly introduce a sick lizard to existing pet reptiles, they may become infected too.

The other problem with animals from mass breeders sold by large pet stores is that the lizards have not been socialized at all, and the salespeople often do not have adequate knowledge or understanding of the creatures they sell. This means that the lack of adequate care continues, *and* the customer is not given the information they require.

HELPFUL TIP
Reptile Super Show

The Reptile Super Show is one of the largest reptile expos in the United States and occurs several times a year. This show is dedicated to working with responsible breeders and vendors to give the public access to exotic reptiles and related gear. Education is a core tenet of the Reptile Super Show, where you can meet and speak with reptile experts, exotic pet enthusiasts, and leopard gecko breeders. For more information about this show and upcoming locations, visit www.reptilesupershow.com.

Exotic Pet Stores

> *I would first recommend looking up the different color morphs and using the patterns that you like to help narrow down the specific gecko for you. 'Fancy' is not a morph but an umbrella term for animals whose genetics have not been properly tracked. I recommend shopping at a quality small local pet shop that's passionate about its animals. That way, you can meet the animals, get a sense of the shop's level of knowledge, and see how the owners run their operations.*
>
> PATRICK KAMBEROS
> *Cold Blooded and Bizarre*

An alternative option to big-chain pet stores is smaller, exotic pet stores that may be in your area. These family-owned businesses take great pride in confirming their animals are healthy, and the stores are held accountable to ensure the preservation of their reputation. Many of these stores have been around for years, and they tend to care about the critters they sell.

I worked in a store like that as my first job. Part of my job was to take time out of the day to handle the reptiles so they would be used to human touch. This is not something that is done in big-chain stores, but it is incredibly helpful to new pet owners as the "hard part" (getting geckos to trust humans) is already taken care of.

Often at these outlets, the store owners breed animals themselves, or they have very strong relationships with reputable breeders. In my experience, the breeders they choose to purchase from are small-scale, old friends, or people whose reptiles have had babies by accident and are sold at the store once they are the appropriate size and confirmed healthy. This ensures they are going to a good home.

It was also my job to make sure people knew how to take proper care of their geckos or other pets and had all the equipment they needed for their animals to live long, happy lives. Choosing the correct food is easy at pet shops like the one I worked at because they always carry everything the animals need. Small shop owners tend to be more caring and offer accurate advice on the animal's care. It is ideal for a reptile owner to be able to establish a long-term relationship with a caring expert.

Often small-scale shops are also willing to order things. For example, if you are looking for a specific type of substrate or tank size they do not have on the shelves, they will often order it for you. They will make every effort to get a hold of a particular morph, too, if that is what a customer wants. It is great to shop locally, but it's even better when you know the animals are cared for, healthy, loved, handled, and you have someone to go back to if something goes wrong.

Breeders

> *I work very closely with potential owners to match them up with the right gecko based on experience, age, and location. From a breeder's perspective, it is important to understand if there will be small children around the animal or if the animal will be mostly kept in a cage since different personalities of geckos will do better in different environments. When adopting through breeders, you can have much more confidence that the animal is healthy and more about the pedigree is known. We go back as far as four generations to understand the lineage of our animals.*
>
> TWYLA GROSS
> *Dakota Geckos*

Small-scale breeders can be a great substitute for purchasing animals at a store. These individuals are professional and knowledgeable and will be there if you have problems or questions. Many good options can be found by doing a Google search and through digital marketplaces

like Facebook. Although you may pay more to buy from a breeder, it is usually worth it.

There are also various Facebook groups you can join to learn more about caring for leopard geckos and connect with people in your area. One good forum is *Fauna Classifieds* which has been around for many years, and I have made successful purchases from it. There are many different breeders available, so contacting multiple sources and getting information is the best way to narrow it down. Groups on social media and forums on the internet are helpful for learning about new advances in animal care and sharing your experiences with other pet owners.

I am also a part of some rehoming groups for my state where people are looking to rehome the animals they own but can no longer keep – for a fee. Most of these reptiles were purchased from breeders, and the current owners can supply where, when, and who they were purchased from.

It is extremely important to do research when buying your pet, and checking out reviews is essential for knowing the animal you are getting is healthy and the breeder is trustworthy. Some ways to prevent an unsuccessful purchase are to contact gecko owners (from Facebook pages or people you know) and ask them if they can recommend a breeder.

Also, a conscientious breeder should be able to provide references or should have testimonials on their web pages and as part of advertisements. Alternatively, there are reptile expos and shows where breeders can win awards for the quality of their reptiles. This is a great resource, and the winners of these awards can typically be found on the reptile expo's website.

Many colleagues of mine breed animals as a hobby. This is not something they do for money. Rather, they enjoy spending time with their geckos and providing them with the care necessary for successful breeding. They care deeply about these creatures as they have nurtured them from eggs, and they may often have requirements before they are willing to send an animal to you.

It is not uncommon for a reputable breeder to ask you for a picture of your enclosure set-up and a list of your diet plan before allowing you to purchase. This indicates to them that you are serious about being a responsible owner. They take great pride in their ability to breed their reptiles, and they strive for the best quality as it provides evidence that they are successful in their hobby and ability to provide the best care.

Photo Courtesy of Jason Gallant Rustic Mountain Reptiles

Naturally, they want to ensure their geckos are going to a home where they will be cared for.

Being that they care so much about these animals, breeders are almost always available for guidance if you contact them after a purchase. I have spoken to several breeders I have purchased from to ask questions about changing diet, enclosure size, and behaviors that I notice. They have always been extremely helpful and supportive. Buying from a breeder is often a much easier and less stressful experience overall. Not only do you get an animal that is healthy and used to being handled, but you get ongoing support.

Successful breeders need a strong understanding of genetics to get the desired morph (color pattern) in their geckos. These little creatures come in so many different colors, and by buying from a breeder, you can learn their lineage in case you want to start breeding them yourself. You will also know what sex and morph your new gecko is. This information is important and helpful, and you won't get it from large pet stores.

Another benefit of purchasing from a breeder is that you are not limited by local availability. You can select the exact morph of gecko you want and have it shipped right to your door. This is incredibly helpful to people who live in remote places and do not have access to exotic pet stores but are still very interested in the hobby. Any professional, reputable breeder will be able to safely package and ship your gecko to you. However, shipping comes with pros and cons.

Sometimes there are weather limitations, and breeders are unable to ship due to temperatures. It is very important for breeders to track temperatures on the route the animal is traveling and at the final destination so the geckos do not get sick from overheating or freezing. In some cases, seasonal weather will require you to pick up your new pet from the nearest package facility to ensure your gecko is not weathering the elements on your front porch.

If the breeder selected is not the best, they will not concern themselves with this and may ship improperly. This could lead to excess stress along your gecko's journey, which can ultimately cause illness or injury. So, do your research on the breeder and pick someone you trust, as it can be vital to the health of your pet.

Chapter 2: Where to Get Your Leopard Gecko

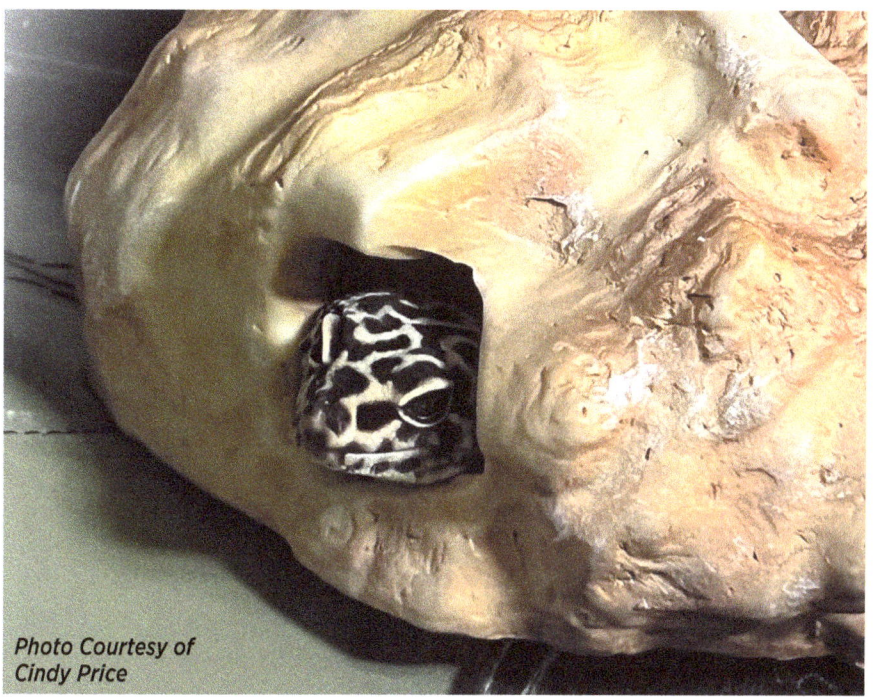

Photo Courtesy of Cindy Price

Lizard & Reptile Shows

Lizard shows or reptile expos or conventions can be an awesome way to meet multiple reputable breeders. These shows are typically held in convention centers, and breeders from all over the country gather to show and sell their animals.

These events are fun for all, and they are a great way to develop a relationship with a breeder before deciding to make a purchase from them. It is also a fantastic way to meet more people in your area who have the same interests as you. Other leopard gecko owners will be present, and becoming a part of that community can help you gain knowledge and make friends on social media with whom you can share information. These pet owners can be an excellent resource for you, and it is wonderful to become part of this community.

Some popular expos available throughout the year are listed in the table below, but there are typically shows in every state:

Name	Location
Sacramento Reptile Show	Sacramento, CA
Loveland Reptile Expo	Loveland, CO
Repticon Orlando Show	Orlando, FL
Repticon	Sarasota, FL
Grovetown Reptile Expo	Grovetown, GA
Iowa Reptile Show	West Des Moines, IA
Lafayette Reptile Expo	Lafayette, IN
Kansas City Reptile Show	Overland Park, KS
Shelbyville Reptile Show	Shelbyville, KY
Repticon Baltimore	Baltimore, MD
Battlefield Reptile Expo	Westminster, MD
Repticon Charlotte	Concord, NC
New England Reptile Expo	Manchester, NH
Capital District Reptile Expo	Albany, NY
Long Island Reptile Expo	Brentwood, NY
Mid-Hudson Reptile Expo	Poughkeepsie, NY
Saratoga Reptile Expo	Saratoga, NY
White Plains Reptile Expo	White Plains, NY
Toledo Reptile Show	Toledo, OH
Portland Metro Reptile Expo	Portland, OR
Altoona Reptile Expo	Altoona, PA
Mid-Atlantic Reptile Expo-Carlisle	Carlisle, PA
Erie Reptile Expo	Erie, PA
Battlefield Reptile Expo	Gettysburg, PA
Hamburg Reptile Expo	Hamburg, PA
York County Reptile Show	York, PA
Northern Virginia Reptile Show	Manassas, VA
Richmond Reptile Expo	Richmond, VA

It is important to plan and prepare before attending one, though. You should do some research so you are informed and not going in without any knowledge of these little reptiles. In addition, you should know what morph or morphs you are interested in, what reputable breeders will be present at the event, which breeders you may want to speak with and have a diet plan ready to go that you can show to breeders who ask for one before selling you a gecko.

At-a-Glance Fact Sheet

- Do some reading about Leopard Geckos.
- Research the stores in your area that sell reptiles.
- Decide if you want to go the pet store or the breeder route to acquire your lizard.
- Carefully investigate the reputation of the pet stores in your area.
- Identify reputable small, specialist, exotic pet stores you could purchase from.
- Investigate the breeders you could use by checking out their reviews and testimonials.
- Approach breeders to discuss your options.
- Attend reptile shows or conventions to meet breeders and other reptile owners.
- Prepare to attend a convention.

CHAPTER 3

Choosing Your Perfect Leopard Gecko

Once you have decided on the breeder or store you want to purchase your new pet from, there are other factors to take into consideration. Some will be more important to you than others. For example, you may not care how old your gecko is.

However, there are certain factors that are paramount: physical and behavioral health. This chapter will help you know what to look for and provide some guidance so you can make more informed decisions about sex, age, and so on.

Choose a Healthy-Looking Gecko

> *Always choose a leopard gecko with a tail that is relative in size to the rest of the animal's body. A nice thick tail is indicative of a healthy animal.*
>
> — STEPHANIE DILLON
> *Granite State Geckos*

Choosing a healthy leopard gecko is the most crucial factor when selecting your pet. This should precede color, sex, age, or any other

Chapter 3: Choosing Your Perfect Leopard Gecko

Photo Courtesy of
Natalie Wittenbrook

characteristic because if your gecko is not healthy, you may end up spending copious amounts of money at the vet, or your gecko may die prematurely. There are plenty of ways to determine if a gecko is healthy.

This will be discussed in greater detail in a later chapter, but there are some initial physical signs that can help you pick a vigorous gecko:

- Healthy leopard geckos should have plump bellies.
- Their tail should be thick, fleshy, and proportionate to the body. Their tail is where they store fat, so having a thick tail means the gecko is metabolizing its food properly.
- A healthy young gecko will also look bright and alert. Its eyes should be clear and follow stimuli.
- The lizard reacts to touch.
- It should be able to walk easily and without its belly touching the ground.
- There are no deformities in the jaw or limbs, there are no missing toes, and the spine is straight.

There are some signs in young leopard geckos that will make it clear right away that it is not healthy.

- A skinny tail could mean the lizard is underfed or has parasites or other health problems.
- Dull eyes with irregular eyelids.
- Drooping head or limbs.
- A gaping mouth.
- Difficulty breathing.
- Stuck shed (where the shed skin has not come off fully or easily).
- Lethargy, little or no movement, and limited or eye responses are cause for concern.
- A dragging belly, which indicates obesity, as this can increase the chances of cysts and heart disease.
- Vomiting and/or diarrhea.

If you are unsure about the way leopard geckos should look, there are numerous photos and many very helpful diagrams available online that give the ideal body shape. It is strongly recommended that you do some research on the morph you are interested in, as some are prone to certain genetic health issues.

For example, the Lemon Frost gene has been linked to cancer, and the Enigma gene can result in neurological issues. If you cannot find information on a specific morph, speak to the breeder, who will be able to provide you with genetic information on the morph/s they breed and sell.

FUN FACT
Leopard Gecko Morphs

Leopard geckos are commonly yellow with black spots, but these popular lizards can be found with many different morphs or color variations. The most common morphs are high yellow, blizzard, tangerine, carrot tail, and lavender. One of the rarest leopard gecko morphs is the Black Night morph, which results in a black body with a yellow belly and can cost around $1,000.

Choose a Gecko Showing Normal, Healthy Behavior

> "You should physically inspect the gecko to make sure it has clear eyes and a thick tail and doesn't have a stuck shed. It should be alert.
>
> MICHAEL EDELEN
> *Cold Blooded and Bizarre*

Selecting a gecko based on its exhibiting healthy, normal behaviors can be challenging as it is not always easy to see in a single visit. If you can visit a gecko multiple times before selecting your pet, this can be much better because you will have more information on how the gecko behaves.

It is always advisable to be on the lookout for geckos that have a good appetite, move effortlessly and smoothly, react to being touched, and react to movements inside and outside of the tank (especially when they are hungry). It is good if they approach the front glass when they are hungry and a caregiver is in sight. These are all signs of healthy young geckos.

Everybody has their bad days, and that goes for lizards too! Do not get discouraged if your young gecko is a bit flighty. It may take some time for them to get used to being handled by humans and by you specifically, but by the time it is an adult, your pet will be calm and cool.

Photo Courtesy of Christie Conley

What Sex, Size, Number, and Age to Choose?

> *I would not recommend putting leopard geckos in pairs. Leopard geckos are very solitary animals and generally do better on their own than in groups. Males are extremely territorial, so if another male is in the cage, they will often fight, sometimes even to the death. Females can sometimes get along in small groups, but it's not recommended.*
>
> SEAN BERGMAN
> *E-ville Geckos*

Selecting a gecko can be a little overwhelming when there are so many options in terms of sex, age, and size. And is a single, a pair, or multiple lizards better?

Some people believe female geckos are less aggressive, but there is no actual data that supports this. At the end of the day, choosing between a male and a female is based on your personal preference. Being that geckos are egg-laying creatures, the females tend to have a shorter life span than the males because egg-laying takes a big toll on the body. Eggs tend to pull nutrients from the females' bodies that male geckos can keep, optimizing their growth, development, and health. Either way, when selecting any reptile, it is important to avoid runts. Although they are cute and tiny, they have the least chance of a long, healthy life. Choosing a big, strong gecko will put you in a better position to start your care routine.

It can be tempting to purchase two – or more – geckos, and some experts feel they do well in multiples, but the bulk of data collected suggests they do better by themselves. These lizards are solitary by nature, and, no, there is no indication or evidence they get lonely. After all, in the wild, they chose to live solitary lives except for brief interactions to fight off a rival or to mate.

If you do opt for multiple geckos, it is not a good idea to place them in the same tank. Even if they appear to be getting on, this can suddenly change, and they may injure each other, potentially seriously. If you have several of these pets and they are housed separately, you can let them interact in a neutral territory outside their habitats. Just be sure to keep an eye on them to make sure everything is going well. Breeding pairs of leopard geckos will be discussed in a later chapter.

Geckos can be purchased at an incredibly early age. If they are moving, eating, and pooping on their own, they are good to go! Most breeders wait until they are six weeks old. At pet stores, they are typically sold a bit older, at the age of four to 12 months. Interestingly, like all reptiles, leopard geckos go on growing for their whole lives! They grow quickly in the first year of their lives, at which point they are considered "full size" because future growth is so minute it is not even noticeable.

Photo Courtesy of Amelia Dare

Keep in mind that you can get the bonding process started when you are checking out the leopard geckos for sale. Some people may find it challenging to believe a bond can be created between a human and a reptile, but, in my experience, it is one of the best bonds there can be. I have selected many of my pets from interactions we have had *before* purchasing.

DID YOU KNOW? A Practical Tail

Leopard geckos have the fascinating ability to detach their tails when bitten by a predator. It takes around 30 days for them to regrow a tail—faster than any other type of lizard.

Sometimes one gecko will come up to the glass and interact with you while you're browsing through a store, or, out of a clutch of bred geckos, one will be more inclined to walk right up your arm. Although it can be difficult to explain to someone who has never bonded with a reptile, it happens, and it's special. When the gecko becomes a part of your family, memories made with it can become family lore for years to come.

Another way your gecko can become a part of the family is by choosing a name for it together. By choosing a name that expresses your gecko's personality, even the most apprehensive members of your family will find themselves falling in love with the creature's individualistic quirks and lovable grin. Spending family time with your gecko creates moments for bonding with all involved. Take lots of photos, especially if you purchase a baby, as you will be able to look at those memories years later when your gecko is a happy, healthy adult.

Also, be sure to celebrate your gecko! It is not always known what day they were born, exactly, but breeders will often have a "hatch date" in their records that you can request. If this information is not available, a suitable alternative is to have a "homecoming day" to celebrate the day you brought home your new family member. Make your gecko a special treat of snacks that fits its diet, and get the whole family involved. This can be a fantastic opportunity for a party, and it makes your gecko a distinguished part of your family!

At-a-Glance Fact Sheet

- Examine the gecko carefully to look for any signs of physical ill health.
- Observe the gecko's behavior to ensure there are no signs of problems.
- Choose whether you want to purchase a male or a female.
- Decide whether you want to own one or more of these lizards, keeping in mind you require a separate tank and equipment for each gecko.
- Your leopard gecko should become part of your family.

CHAPTER 4

Leopard Gecko Morphs

Introduction to Morphs

Some level of diversity is a constant in most species throughout our planet. For leopard geckos, which have been selected and bred by humans for decades, this is especially true. In the reptile pet trade, a common name for these different phenotypes is morphs. A morph is a particular physical variant of an animal. The word is especially used to describe differences in coloration. Other physical characteristics, like size or other physical features, are also often described as morphs. Because of this, animals can sometimes display multiple morphs simultaneously or exhibit some combination of morphs. Some morphs may be subtle, while others are incredibly visually striking. Some morphs look similar but may be caused by entirely different genes.

Importance of morphs in leopard gecko breeding and the pet trade

Morphs in leopard geckos and other pet reptiles are important in determining the animal's cost. Newer or rarer morphs can end up costing buyers a pretty penny. There are as many as 150 morphs in leopard geckos, up from just a dozen or so a few decades ago. In recent years, the morph market has exploded, and new physical characteristics, color patterns, and crosses are being discovered every day. Most of the new morphs are a result of crossbreeding and expansion on previously existing morphs.

How morphs are created (genetics and inheritance)

Leopard geckos, and most animals, have two copies of each gene in their DNA. Each leopard gecko parent provides one copy of each gene. Many morphs originate as genetic mutations, through different morphs are passed on in different ways. Later in the chapter, we will discuss the different ways these traits can be inherited.

Ethical considerations in breeding and purchasing morphs

Like any living things, leopard geckos require certain conditions and environments to survive and thrive. In captivity, responsible owners will often do their best to meet these requirements by simulating their pets' ideal natural environment and lifestyle. On the other hand,

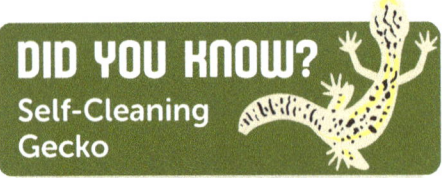

DID YOU KNOW?
Self-Cleaning Gecko

A healthy adult leopard gecko will shed every four to eight weeks, while babies and juveniles shed more frequently. This shed is more than a protective layer; it also contains valuable vitamins and minerals. For this reason, leopard geckos typically eat their shed as it detaches from their body. Not only does this practice help leopard geckos retain essential nutrients, but it's also a survival tactic. In the wild, the scent of the shed can lure predators to the leopard gecko's den.

breeders are often incentivized to produce as many leopard geckos as possible, with the smallest overhead costs, in the shortest time frame. This often leads to inadequate and unsafe practices in breeding leopard geckos. Unfortunately, some morphs are the result of this or are more likely to suffer health problems as a result. Inbreeding has led to several morphs being more prone to certain genetic diseases than others. In other cases, breeders have taken to irresponsible practices in order to exaggerate the features of certain morphs.

One example, Giant or Super Giant leopard geckos are morphs characterized by their unusually large size, sometimes exceeding 100 grams. Breeders who want to emphasize their geckos' size may overfeed them and cause them to become obese. Sometimes even regular obese leopard geckos are passed off as Giants. The Lemon Frost morph, first bred in 2015, often grows cancerous skin lesions and tumors throughout its body. As a result, it's unlikely to live a full life span, usually dying within two years of hatching. Lemon Frost and the similarly troubled Enigma morph are both banned from being displayed at shows hosted by the International Herpetological Society. Noir Désir is a morph from 2013 that can have eye deformities and possible fertility issues in its super strain.

No responsible pet owners want to see their animals suffer. The above examples illustrate some of the reasons why leopard gecko owners should dedicate some consideration and attention when purchasing certain morphs.

Chapter 4: Leopard Gecko Morphs

Terminology Associated with Morphs

Wild-type (normal) leopard gecko

Wild-type is the standard coloration found among leopard geckos in their native Central Asian habitat. Most leopard geckos you encounter will be wild type. Wild-type leopard geckos are mostly yellow with a white underside, and covered in black spots. This color pattern, reminiscent of a certain African and Asian big cat, is where the leopard gecko name originates.

Genes and alleles relevant to morphs

Some traits are brought on by multiple genes, known as polygenic traits, while others are single-gene traits. Jungles, Stripes, Tangerines, and Bandits are some famous polygenic morphs. Polygenic traits can present in much more varied ways from individual to individual, and these traits are often selected for over generations of leopard geckos. Single-gene trait morphs include White and Yellows, and Enigmas. The particular genes associated with a morph are known in some cases and not in others, especially in the case of polygenic traits.

Heterozygous vs. homozygous morphs

A homozygous trait has two of the same gene alleles, either both dominant or both recessive. If the alleles are different, one dominant and one recessive, the animal is considered heterozygous. In single-gene morphs, a heterozygous animal will present the trait associated with the dominant allele, while still being able to pass the hidden recessive allele on to its offspring. A pairing between two homozygous dominant individuals will result in all homozygous-dominant offspring. A pairing between two homozygous-recessive individuals will result in all homozygous-recessive offspring. A pairing between two heterozygous individuals will produce approximately 25% homozygous-dominant, 50% heterozygous, and 25% homozygous-recessive offspring. A pairing between a homozygous and heterozygous individual will result in half of the offspring being homozygous and the other half heterozygous.

Co-dominant vs. recessive morphs

Homozygous co-dominant genes, unlike standard homozygous traits, will produce individuals that present different characteristics from heterozygous individuals. Co-dominant genes often produce a more extreme version of a trait, or even a different trait entirely, when two copies of the allele are present. Reptiles expressing homozygous co-dominance are often called supers.

Morphs that rely on recessive genes require that both parents be homozygous recessive to produce all recessive offspring. The introduction of a dominant allele will override recessive copies of a gene. Recessive morphs can only be produced by two recessive-dominant individuals.

Mack Snows and Giants are two examples of co-dominant morphs, while Blizzards, Patternlesses, and Eclipses are all brought on by recessive alleles.

Lineage and genealogy tracking

Genealogy is important to keep up with when breeding leopard gecko morphs. Responsible breeders will record the known genetics of all their geckos in order to predict the most likely outcome when breeding any two individuals. Failing to record your leopard gecko's genetics may result in unexpressed genes being unintentionally passed on to the next generation, which could have undesirable outcomes for anyone trying to produce a particular morph or cross.

The Most Common Leopard Gecko Morphs

- **Albino**

Albino leopard geckos are actually the result of three separate mutations. The Tremper, Rainwater, and Bell lines all have a signature albinistic look, with some minor differences. Because they're the result of three different mutations, breeding together different albino strains will result in heterozygous wild-type offspring. Albinos are prone to light sensitivity, vision problems, and skin cancer when exposed to UV rays.

Albino Bell   *Albino Rainwater*   *Albino Tremper*

- **Blizzard**

Blizzards are mostly white or off-white morphs. Their light coloration and lack of pattern make them a popular canvas for crossing with other morphs. Some Blizzard crosses, like the Mack Snow Blizzard, are said to have a tendency toward over-aggression.

Blizzard

- **Hypomelanistic (super hypo)**

Hypomelanistic morphs display less black coloration on their body. A common rule of thumb is less than 10% of their body can contain dark colors.

Hypomelanistic

Chapter 4: Leopard Gecko Morphs

- **Tangerine**

Tangerine leopard geckos often have vibrant orange or tangerine hues to varying degrees. While some may express orange coloration throughout the body, others may be limited to just sections.

Tangerine

- **Mack Snow**

Mack Snows have a white base with black spots throughout much of the body. They will often also have black eyes, despite not having the Eclipse gene. While normal leopard geckos can be temperature-sexed, Mack Snows are not as consistent in this regard.

Mack Snow

- **Eclipse**

Eclipse refers to a leopard gecko morph with all-black eyes. Instead of the typical iris pigmentation, the pupil of the eclipse is indistinguishable from the rest of the eye. Eclipse eyes can sometimes take on a red appearance due to the presence of blood vessels. It is a recessive trait and is often found in conjunction with other morphs.

Eclipse

- **Jungle**

The Jungle morph is made up of leopard geckos with irregular, broken, or incomplete spot patterns.

Jungle

- **Enigma**

Enigmas are controversial morphs because of the severe neurological issues that are prevalent in their bloodline. Enigma syndrome will cause the head to uncontrollably tilt back—a phenomenon called stargazing—along with seizures and spinning. Enigmas will often have poor balance and coordination. This can make feeding difficult and often does not lead to them having a healthy weight or appetite.

The low quality of life and increased level of care Enigmas require have made their breeding generally looked down upon in many pet trade circles and has caused the morph to be banned by organizations like the International Herpetological Society, as mentioned earlier.

Enigma

Chapter 4: Leopard Gecko Morphs

- **High Yellow**

One of the first designer traits, High Yellows have a reduced spot pattern and a greater percentage of yellow on their bodies.

High Yellow

- **RAPTOR (Red-Eyed Patternless Tremper Orange)**

RAPTORs are red-eyed albino geckos with orange-colored bodies. They are a combination of the Eclipse, Patternless Stripe, and Tremper Albino morph.

Raptor

- **SHTCT (Super Hypo Tangerine Carrot Tail)**

The SHTCT is a combination morph. This morph is characterized by a lack of body spots, orange coloration covering at least 15% or so of the tail, and tangerine-like coloration on their bodies.

SHTCT

- **Super Snow**

Super Snows are the super form of the Mack Snow and other Snow morphs. This morph will have a more striking and consistent stark-white base color with the potential for reduced black spots. Super Snows are sometimes said

Super Snow

to be more likely to have facial deformities, grow more slowly, and be underweight.

- **W&Y (White and Yellow)**

W&Ys often have high white sides, a large white band on the nape of the neck, dorsal striping, bright white tails, high-contrast colors, and faded and reduced spotting. Some White and Yellows may be more prone to balance problems and wobbling.

W&Y

- **Gem Snow**

Gem Snows have a white body with dark spots. They are related to the Mack Snow and have a chance of producing Super Snow offspring when bred with other Snow morphs.

Gem Snow

- **Diablo Blanco**

The Diablo Blanco is a stark white and patternless leopard gecko with red-hued eyes.

Diablo Blanco

- **Patternless**

Patternless leopard geckos have few to no spots on their body.

Patternless

- **Lavender**

A polygenic trait, Lavender leopard geckos will have a light violet hue that may become more difficult to spot as the reptile ages.

Lavender

- **Ghost**
Ghosts have faded coloration, especially in regard to spots and darker colors.

Ghost

- **Carrot Tail**
Carrot Tails often have vibrant orange coloration running down the base of their tails.

- **TUG Snow (Tremper Ultra-melanistic Ghost)**
TUG Snows have little to no yellow coloration and often have reduced patterns.

TUG Snow

Rarity and Pricing

Rarity levels in leopard gecko morphs

There is a significant level of variety in how common some morphs might be compared to others. New morphs and crosses are created every year. Some morphs are commonly found anywhere leopard geckos are sold, while others may only be accessible through specific breeders. One of the contenders for the rarest morph is the Black Night leopard gecko, which can cost anywhere between $1200 and $4000. The Black Night leopard gecko is the result of a genetic condition called melanism, meaning it produces excessive amounts of pigment, often resulting in a black or near-black lizard. The Black Night may contain some shades of brown and other colors in spots or patches. A newer morph, the Black

Pearl, is even more melanistic than the Black Night. They are not yet largely available to the public, but at least one female has been sold at auction for $3000.

Factors influencing the pricing of morphs

A wild-type leopard gecko might cost as little as $20 to $40. Rarer morphs can cost hundreds or even thousands of dollars. Often, rarer morphs, especially those that have visually striking or unique features, will cost much more than more common morphs. The difficulty involved and the time it takes to breed the traits that characterize certain morphs will also impact rarity and cost.

Recognizing valuable and unique morph combinations

When trying to gauge how valuable a morph might be, striking visuals and the level of difficulty associated with creating said morph are going to be major factors. When presented with any uncertainty, do your research on that particular morph and reach out to sellers, owners, and breeders within the leopard gecko community.

CHAPTER 5

The Perfect Vivarium

It is, as mentioned earlier, very important that you have your new leopard gecko's habitat ready before you bring it home to begin its new life with you and your family. This will make the transition much less stressful for both pets and people.

Your new family member and buddy will need a range of items, including the correct size tank, a suitable lamp or ceramic heat emitter, lighting, a thermometer, thermostat, a water bowl, suitable and safe substrate, décor items, hides (although you can make your own), and the necessary supplements.

Welcoming Your Leopard Gecko Home

> *In the first weeks after you bring your new gecko home, it will need time to acclimate to the new environment. I cannot stress enough the importance of leaving the gecko alone and not handling it, except when necessary, during this time. While it is getting acclimated, the gecko will spend a lot of time in hiding and will not begin feeding until it starts to feel comfortable. Do not panic; a healthy gecko can go weeks without food. Make sure the habitat temperatures are appropriate, provide access to food and water, and just give your new time to minimize its stress level.*
>
> MARK BRUNSDON
> *CAN Geckos*

Chapter 5: The Perfect Vivarium

One of the best parts of purchasing a leopard gecko is bringing it home and making it comfortable! Developing and designing the enclosure can be so much fun, but it is important to remember the reptile's needs when doing so. If the habitat is set up before purchasing the gecko, you can check that everything is functioning properly so you can put your new pet in it and prevent it from spending unnecessary time in the carry-home container without proper heating. Geckos have a better chance of settling in quickly if everything is ready to go for them upon arrival.

When developing a gecko's habitat, try to keep the decor and temperature as close to the reptile's natural habitat as possible. By recreating what a gecko would encounter in the wild, you not only have an amazing pet but a little piece of another part of the world in your home! It can be tempting to deck the tank out with lots of decorations, but always remember to put the safety and well-being of your gecko first. Having a pretty habitat can be achieved without using potentially dangerous elements. We will be more specific later in the chapter.

Vivarium Options

> *When getting any new animal, you're bound to make mistakes. The key is to learn from them, ask questions, and be willing to make changes that will benefit your new friend in the long run. You should never consider yourself an expert, because care standards are always changing and evolving. You may change your enclosure many times before finding the perfect setup for you and your gecko. Don't forget that leopard geckos can live well into their thirties if they receive proper lifelong care, so they are a long-term commitment.*
>
> DYLAN AND SAM JONES
> *Galactic Reptiles*

The most common vivarium option is aquarium tanks. These can be made of glass, acrylic plastic, and sometimes even wood. The size is important as it ensures your gecko has enough room to exercise, explore, and have an enriching hunting experience.

Geckos must be kept in a 10-gallon tank at a minimum, but a 20-gallon tank is better. Although it is not recommended, if you decide to keep more than one gecko in the same tank together, add five gallons to the tank size for every additional gecko. Therefore, if you start at a 10-gallon tank and get another gecko, the minimum size tank should be 15 gallons. Your geckos will benefit from having more room to explore, so give them the space if possible.

When selecting your tank, it is better to choose low, long tanks rather than high, tall ones. Leopard geckos are not tree climbers and will not use tall spaces. Getting a long, low tank will provide your gecko with ample walking space and opportunities for burrowing.

Often there is a choice between a glass top, acrylic top, or screen top for the enclosure's lid. Screen tops are the best option for leopard geckos because they increase airflow, preventing mold and mildew. The lid is not

Chapter 5: The Perfect Vivarium

Photo Courtesy of Madison Brown

necessarily required for keeping your leopard geckos in the tank as they cannot climb walls, but it will protect them from curious cats, dogs, birds, and children that may accidentally hurt them. There are also special tank locks available that prevent the lid from opening. They slide over the edge of a screen lid and click firmly into place along the plastic border. This is great for childproofing if there are young children who need supervision when holding the gecko.

Geckos can be sneaky climbers on the decor in their tanks. If you do not have a lid, they may be able to find a way out using their hides or decorative sticks as ladders. Screen lids are also the best for supporting a heat lamp if you decide to use one. The specific heating requirements are described later.

However, screen tops are not always the best for access, especially if you have a heat lamp resting on them, as lifting the lid means the heat lamp must be removed first. It can be challenging to move the heat lamp to the right spot because the bulb is easily shattered and is extremely hot. If you rest it on wood or carpeting while opening the tank, it can be a serious fire hazard. The company Exoterra, among others, makes beautiful, front-opening enclosures with built-in screen tops.

There are several reasons why front-opening tanks are a good choice. First, approaching your gecko from the front can prevent a stress

Chapter 5: The Perfect Vivarium

response. Most natural predators, like birds, attack the geckos from above. Grabbing your gecko from a top-access tank can startle it, causing distress and even a bite. In addition, front-opening tanks are easier to clean and get into, but you should never leave the doors open for ventilation because it is much easier for a gecko to escape from tanks that open this way. If you are hoping to keep young children from opening the tank on their own, there are locks sold with a turn-number password. Most front-opening tanks have a little hole where the door grips meet to lock both doors securely.

Broadly speaking, there are three options in terms of material: glass, plastic (acrylic/PVC), or wood. Each material offers the owner or gecko both advantages and disadvantages

Glass Tanks
Pros

- Easy to clean
- Sold in any pet store and discounted at certain times
- Easy to find secondhand
- Watertight
- Safe for high heat and supports overhead heat lamps
- Great longevity
- Provides a better thermal gradient so your gecko can change temperatures within the tank as it pleases
- Looks good for display

Glass Tanks
Cons

- Breakable
- Older models are very heavy
- Needs locks to keep lids on for top opening tank
- Clear walls can allow for too much visibility, stressing your gecko out. This can be fixed using paper to block the sides and back. Special backgrounds can also be purchased.
- They do not hold heat or humidity as well; they are not well insulated.

Plastic Tanks (PVC/Acrylic) Pros

- ✓ Lightweight
- ✓ Cheaper than some other alternatives
- ✓ Supports a heat lamp under the lid
- ✓ Maintains heat and humidity well
- ✓ Most are front-opening and stackable.
- ✓ Usually, three out of four sides are dark, which reduces stress on your pet.

Plastic Tanks (PVC/Acrylic) Cons

- ✗ Plastic can get scratched and foggy after a while, reducing visibility.
- ✗ High heat may melt the plastic; overhead lamps are not supported.
- ✗ Plastic can crack easily, so it is not always watertight.
- ✗ Lighting must be mounted inside the tank, increasing the risk of burns to your reptile without the use of wire-bulb cages.
- ✗ Typically have less ventilation unless additional holes are drilled.

Photo Courtesy of Ashley Bryant

Chapter 5: The Perfect Vivarium

Wood Tanks
Pros

- Natural look and is more aesthetically pleasing if displaying your pet in living areas
- Inexpensive and can be created yourself
- Endless customizations and easy-to-make changes

Wood Tanks
Cons

- High heat can be a fire hazard as wood is flammable.
- If not sealed properly, wood can absorb moisture and cause mold and mildew. This can cause health issues in your gecko.
- Heavy
- Splintering/chipping can prevent them from lasting as long as glass tanks.
- Wood is porous, so it can absorb bacteria. Proper sanitization can be difficult.

If you find this decision confusing and difficult, you can ask for advice from a breeder or other owners via a forum. It is also a matter of personal taste, practicality in terms of your life circumstances, and budget. Note, too, that a reptile starter kit is not a good option, as your lizard will outgrow it quickly. It is far better to begin with a good-sized tank that will make a good home for the rest of your gecko's life. There are detailed discussions of tank setups and requirements later in this chapter.

Where to Put the Tank

You must also put thought into the placement of your leopard gecko's tank in your home. Selecting the best place for it will prevent unwanted stress on your pet and increase your involvement with it. There are several useful general guidelines.

Firstly, you should keep the tank in a safe and secure spot that is out of the way so that it is not easily bumped into or damaged. Secondly, it is helpful to keep geckos at eye level so you can easily monitor – and enjoy – their activity while moving through your home during the day. Finally, because leopard geckos do not get fed daily, it can be easy to forget about them if they are kept out of sight and you are not interacting with them regularly for other reasons. Importantly, they are very curious and inquisitive animals, and they enjoy watching the activity in the house.

I believe that keeping your geckos where they can watch peaceful activity makes them a bit more sociable. It is best to keep them out of reach of small children and pets and out of direct sunlight. Too much sun can overheat your gecko or cause sunburn in albino morphs. Indirect, ambient light is best. Too much darkness can mess up your gecko's circadian rhythm, disrupting its natural feeding and sleeping cycles.

You may have other pets that are simply curious or want to make friends with your gecko. Others look at a lizard and see a meal or a toy! Either way, you need to protect your gecko, and the best way to do this is to keep the tank away from other pets. There are several ways you can do this:

- Place your tank up high and on a sturdy stand or piece of furniture. If dogs jump up to look at your gecko, this will keep the whole tank from falling over.
- If there is a place in your home your pets do not have access to, that is sometimes the best option. Some pets are very persistent and will stop at nothing to get inside a tank. Keeping geckos behind closed doors is sometimes the only option. Just make sure you keep the tank/s in a space you actively use so you do not forget about your gecko, and it has a chance to observe some activity and/or interact with you.

Chapter 5: The Perfect Vivarium

Photo Courtesy of Mikayla Sullivan

- Use tank locks on screen tops and front-opening enclosures to ensure pets do not gain entry.
- If you are using a heat lamp that is resting on a screen lid, use a lamp lock that secures your lamp to the lid so pets (like cats) do not knock it to the ground. This is important because heat lamps can be a fire hazard.
- If you have persistent cats, placing tinfoil on the surfaces they use to climb up to the tank can deter them and keep them away.

- If possible, teach or train your other pets to respect the tank and to keep their distance.

In summary, the tank should be somewhere safe from human traffic and other pets and where your gecko will have some stimulus but not be overwhelmed or stressed.

How to Clean Your Tank

> *Care routines are actually very minimal. Leopard geckos generally choose a corner of their terrarium to defecate in, making clean-up super easy and quick. If the animal defecates on its hides, you'll want to wash and disinfect those at least weekly, or however often it occurs. Water and food dishes should be washed weekly as well.*
>
> STEPHANIE DILLON
> *Granite State Geckos*

Leopard geckos are naturally fastidious creatures, and they do a wonderful job of keeping themselves and their tank clean. This makes them pretty low maintenance. However, it is still necessary to clean the habitat regularly.

Cleaning your leopard gecko tank should become a daily habit so that you remove feces and urate. Leopards often select a place, sometimes not an easy one to spot, to defecate. Make sure you find it, or your cleaning efforts will not be effective. There are different methods of cleaning, depending on the substrate used. If you use a reptile mat/carpet, a tissue is sufficient for lifting the dirty material from the enclosure. If you are using sand, there are sifters that lift the waste but leave the sand behind, like when scooping a litter box.

Weekly cleaning is needed, particularly if you use loose feeders like crickets. Water and food containers should ideally be cleaned daily but must at least be washed every week to prevent the buildup of dirt and possibly bacteria or mold in what is a warm, humid environment. If the tank also contains live plants, this weekly clean should extend to a light spray of the foliage with water.

Never use conventional cleaners in your tank, as they may leave a residue of chemicals, alcohol, and other synthetic ingredients that could damage your pet's health. Avoid spray cleaners that have heavy scents, as reptiles have a more refined olfactory system than humans do. Soapy water works well, and so does the safe, cheap alternative to chemical cleaners: a white vinegar solution. This is safe for your pet, although the tank should always be rinsed well or wiped down with a wet cloth afterward to remove any remaining traces of vinegar or soap from the surfaces. The vinegar is also a fantastic glass cleaner and will leave a streak-free view for you to see your pet and your gecko to see out. Dilute the vinegar before use, even though it is naturally non-toxic. The correct ratio is 1:1 (or one-part white vinegar to one-part water).

In addition, a thorough cleaning of the whole tank should be done two to four times per month. Scrub the tank with warm soapy water or diluted vinegar. Be sure to rinse and dry the tank thoroughly, so no remnants of cleaning solution are left behind, as these may be toxic to your gecko. Remove all substrate and clean all the tank accessories, too (this will be discussed in the next chapter). Do not forget to wash your hands before and after cleaning and dispose of waste material properly in the trash.

Using checklists can help to remind you of what needs to be done and when:

HELPFUL TIP
When to Handle Hatchlings

Leopard geckos are friendly and popular family pets, but when can you start playing with your brand-new lizard? Experts recommend not handling leopard geckos too frequently as the geckos acclimate to their new habitat. However, once your gecko has reached around six inches long and is comfortable in its new home, you can start playing with it for 10 to 15 minutes daily to build your relationship.

Daily Cleaning Checklist

 Remove all fecal matter and urates.

 Check for mold and mildew under water bowls and under hides, especially in humid hides.

 Make sure no debris has collected on top of the screen under the heat lamp.

 Remove any uneaten food.

 Remove the water bowl, scrub with soapy water, rinse thoroughly, and provide fresh water.

 Check your gecko's skin. If it looks as though it will shed soon (this is indicated by faded, dull colors), provide extra humidity for easier shedding by misting or replacing the moss in the humid hide. If your gecko is actively shedding, place it in a safe, ventilated container with warm water up to its elbows for a 10-minute soak.

 Check your gecko's behavior and temperament to ensure it looks healthy and is acting normally.

 Make sure your tank temperatures are correct by checking the thermostats or using a temperature-reading gun. Also, check the humidity and adjust it as needed.

Monthly Cleaning Checklist (2–4 times a month)

 Remove your gecko from the enclosure and place it in a safe, ventilated, escape-proof container away from pets, small children, and high-traffic areas where the container could get knocked over.

 It can be good to give your gecko a soak in warm water during this time to help with hydration and make shedding easier. Make sure the container is ventilated, and only fill the water level up to your pet's elbows.

 Remove all decor and sanitize it by boiling it in water or cleaning it with soapy water. Live plants should not, of course, be boiled, but leaves can be wiped clean with a soap solution and then rinsed off. All decor must be rinsed well before replacing. If you use a humid hide, replace all moss or water-holding substrate.

 Remove, scrub, and sanitize all water bowls and food dishes. Rinse thoroughly.

 Remove all substrate and dispose of it properly in the trash.

 Scrub the tank with soapy water or diluted vinegar solution.

 Rinse the tank thoroughly to remove any residue.

 Wipe the inside of the tank glass with diluted vinegar to get a streak-free shine.

 Dust the screen top lid. Do not use water on metal screen lids unless it is dried completely, as it can cause rusting.

Photo Courtesy of Natalie Wittenbrook

Chapter 5: The Perfect Vivarium

You may find these checklists useful or prefer to design your own list or spreadsheet that helps you to easily see what needs to be done when.

At-a-Glance Fact Sheet

- Keep the decor and temperature as close to the reptile's natural habitat as possible.
- Set the tank up before purchasing your gecko and check everything is functioning properly.
- A 10-gallon tank is the minimum size, but a 20-gallon tank is better.
- It is better to choose low, long tanks rather than high, tall ones.
- Screen tops are the best option for leopard geckos, and front-opening tanks are a good choice.
- There are three options in terms of tank material: glass, plastic (acrylic/PVC), or wood.
- Put thought into the placement of your leopard gecko's tank so that it is in a safe, secure spot where the gecko can watch peaceful activity but is out of reach of small children and other pets and away from direct sunlight.
- It is necessary to clean the habitat regularly, with certain things being done daily and others weekly.
- Never use conventional cleaners, as they may leave a residue of chemicals, alcohol, and other synthetic ingredients that could damage your pet's health. Use soapy water or white vinegar in a 1:1 ratio with water.

CHAPTER 6

Substrate, Hides, and Decorations

Once you have decided what type of tank your gecko will be housed in and where it will be placed, you also need to select the most appropriate substrate, hides, and decor that will make your gecko feel at home and happy.

Substrate

> *I don't recommend loose substrates. We prefer to use tiles, linoleum, sand mats/paper, paper towels, or newspaper.*
>
> **SEAN BERGMAN**
> *E-ville Geckos*

When developing the habitat for your gecko, it is particularly important to emulate their natural environment as much as possible in their captive habitat.

Fortunately, there are plenty of good natural substrates available that will help you achieve this. Some examples are stone slate, large river pebbles, and excavator clay. Alternatively, there are some non-natural substrates such as paper towels, reptile carpet, newspaper, linoleum, sand mats, sandpaper, and ceramic tiles that are also good options.

Chapter 6: Substrate, Hides, and Decorations

Bad substrates include any loose materials. The most common of these types of substrates are sand, calcium sand, quartz, walnut shell, wood chippings, bark, and other forest substrates. Because these lizards are not graceful hunters, they can easily get a mouthful of substrate along with the insect. Although leopard geckos are found in arid areas, loose substrates such as sand can kill them if consumed, as they can cause fatal impactions within the digestive tract. In fact, this is the leading cause of death in leopard geckos.

Leopard Gecko in loose substrate (sand), Not recommended

Plants

Plants, whether living or fake, are not required in the gecko's enclosure as they are not a significant feature in their natural habitats. They can, of course, be added to make the vivarium more aesthetically pleasing to you, and this can be a fun project to do with the family. However, most people find that real plants cannot thrive in a leopard gecko habitat because there is no natural light and not enough moisture. The exceptions to this are the various species of air plants (*Tillandsia*). Air plants can be attached to the walls or rocks of the enclosure. They should be misted once or twice a week, and they need some degree of sunlight. They can also be beneficial in adding humidity to the gecko's habitat.

Artificial plants can add a great pop of color to your habitat, and the plants chosen are a matter of personal preference. Artificial plants that are very intricate are far more prone to getting dusty, so it can be better to select plants that are less complicated in their structure. It is important

Photo Courtesy of Alyssa Kane

Chapter 6: Substrate, Hides, and Decorations

Photo Courtesy of Rachel Linesburgh

to wash them regularly when doing other maintenance for the tank. Also, if the artificial plants are in the habitat where the gecko can access them, it is important to properly disinfect them before adding them to the enclosure so they do not introduce any bacteria or other microbes or pathogens into the habitat. This can be done in boiling water or using a diluted vinegar soak followed by a thorough rinse and dry.

Hides

A hide is one of the most important elements of your leopard gecko's habitat. It will provide your gecko with a stress-free environment to hide away from the outside world. In the wild, leopard geckos find spots to stay safe and protected during the hours of the day when it is hottest and when most predators are out. If your home is cool, it is necessary to ensure that a heat lamp maintains the required temperature for your gecko.

Hides can be created very easily, but burrows work as well if you want to give your gecko a spot to hide under the substrate level. You can

Photo Courtesy of
Tiffany Sharpeta

use large rocks, a plastic food container turned upside down with a door cut out, or you can purchase a hide specifically designed for reptiles. It is always good to offer your gecko multiple options for hiding spots. The ideal number is three. One should be warm, one cool, and another moist.

- The warm hide should be placed on the side of the tank where the heat lamp or heat pad is located.
- The cool hide should be on the opposite end of the tank from the warm hide.
- The humid hide should be placed in an area of the tank that will hold the most moisture (away from direct heat).

The specifics of the humid hide will be discussed further in a later section.

Chapter 6: Substrate, Hides, and Decorations

> *One of the most initially overlooked supplies that will drastically reduce shedding issues is providing your gecko with a moist hide on the warm side of the enclosure. The moist hide can be as elaborate or as simple as you want. It should have an opening that provides the gecko easy access, but one small enough that the hide can maintain humidity within it. Your moist hide should contain a form of substrate that holds moisture without getting moldy (such as sphagnum moss or coconut fiber), and it should be kept moist at all times.*
>
> MARK BRUNSDON
> *CAN Geckos*

Decorations or Tank Decor

Decorations like rocks, logs, and branches can offer fantastic environmental enrichment for your gecko. Leopard geckos lack the hooks on their feet that help other species climb walls, but logs and rocks to climb can be a wonderful way to inspire your gecko to be active and make their lives more interesting. They can also create shelter. Rougher types of items, such as bark-covered branches or rougher rocks, have the added benefit of keeping your gecko's claws at a good length by wearing them down a little. If claws get too long, they can cause some health issues.

However, you need to be sure that any materials added as decoration are well-secured and firmly attached. If they are

FUN FACT
Funny Feet

Unlike other geckos, leopard geckos do not have sticky pads on their feet. Instead, they have small claws to help them get a grip. For this reason, you won't see leopard geckos scaling smooth walls like Crested and Tokay geckos. Leopard geckos are more likely to enjoy climbing rocks and branches with their uniquely adapted claws.

Photo Courtesy of Jennifer Hammond

too loose, they can fall and injure your gecko. Smooth rocks are much safer, but they can be harder for geckos to climb. It is best to use your judgment and try different options to see what your gecko prefers. It can also be a good idea to watch your lizard for a while after introducing these types of decorations into the tank to check that things look secure and solid when they are being climbed on or explored.

Branches should be placed on the side of the enclosure where the heat lamp is. This will allow your gecko to get closer to the heat during times it wants or needs to warm up. Just be careful that the branches are not too close to the heat source, as your gecko could accidentally burn itself. The best course of action to make sure this does not happen is to place the branches in the tank for a few hours when your gecko is not in it (this is an opportunity to hang out with your pet for a while). Then, use a temperature gun to read the temperature of the highest point of the branch to ensure it is not too hot for your pet.

Chapter 6: Substrate, Hides, and Decorations

Cleaning Substrate and Decor

As mentioned in the previous chapter, be sure to clean everything in the tank at least twice a month. To recap with regards to substrate and decor specifically:

- All the substrate material should be removed and replaced when doing the deep clean every two weeks.

Photo Courtesy of Jennifer Robbins

- Branches and decor should be scrubbed and replaced in a new position to keep your gecko active and alert.

Using the correct materials in the habitat and keeping them clean is crucial. There are other requirements that you must stay on top of to keep your gecko healthy. More on this later!

> *Weekly routines should include supplying fresh insects, supplements, and water. Spot cleaning any excrement should also be included in a weekly schedule. Monthly care should consist of completely cleaning the enclosure, including disinfecting the enclosure and providing new substrate.*
>
> DYLAN AND SAM JONES
> *Galactic Reptiles*

At-a-Glance Fact Sheet

- It is important to emulate their natural environment as much as possible.
- Items like rocks, logs, and branches offer fantastic environmental enrichment.
- Ensure all decor items are secured so that they do not fall and injure your pet.
- You can select either a natural substrate or a non-natural substrate.
- Bad substrates include any loose materials as they can cause impaction.
- Plants are not required but can be added to make the vivarium more attractive.
- Air plants are the best living plant option, and simple artificial plants can be used.

At-a-Glance Fact Sheet ...Continued

- A hide is crucial and provides your gecko with a safe place to hide.
- Three hides are ideal: a warm hide, a cool hide, and a humid hide.
- The substrate, decor, and hides must be kept clean.

CHAPTER 7

Lighting and Humidity

There are several crucial issues that need to be attended to and maintained to keep your leopard gecko healthy – and happy. It is essential to keep in mind the living conditions of these reptiles in the wild and get the temperature and humidity levels right.

Leopard Gecko Heating Needs

> *The most important thing for the leopard gecko setup is the heat source. Leopard geckos require belly heat to digest their food. A heating pad controlled by a thermostat set at 90 degrees Fahrenheit is the simplest and most effective way to provide this.*
>
> **MIKE RICHARD**
> *Maritime Geckos*

In the wild, leopard geckos do not enjoy extremely hot temperatures and sand. They prefer to hide in the shade during the hottest parts of the day. They are often found in desert areas with clay or gravel-mixed soil rather than strictly sand. To create the best habitat for your leopard gecko, try to mimic these attributes as closely as possible.

Leopard geckos are ectothermic, meaning they are cold-blooded, and their body temperature is determined by that of the air and ambient

Chapter 7: Lighting and Humidity

temperature around them. For this reason, it is important to provide a constant temperature and a gradient within the tank so that the gecko can adjust its own temperature as necessary. This gradient can be created by placing the heat source at one end of the tank so that end is the warmest and the air cools gradually toward the opposite end. As mentioned previously, it is crucial that the temperature settings are correct before you place your gecko into the habitat.

Geckos will bask in their hot spot on the warm side whenever they require additional heat. This could be during periods of digestion or part of their daily routine. Once they are sufficiently warm, they will move to the opposite end of the tank to cool down.

Photo Courtesy of
Jennifer Hammond

Thermometer

> *Place your heat source on one end of the enclosure to establish a proper temperature gradient. Make sure that your temperatures are appropriate in the enclosure before introducing the gecko.*
>
> PATRICK KAMBEROS
> *Cold Blooded and Bizarre*

To accurately monitor the temperature of the gecko's enclosure, you must place a thermometer in their tank. There are thermometers specifically sold for reptiles. However, you need to be careful to purchase a good quality one. For instance, the ones that come with reptile or tank kits and the small, adhesive analog thermostats have a reputation for not being accurate at all.

Chapter 7: Lighting and Humidity

Photo Courtesy of Madison Brown

Having two thermometers can be useful for monitoring both the cool side and the warm side of the tank. The optimum daytime temperature for leopard geckos is 75–85°F (24–29°C) during the day, with the basking area going as high as 90°F (32°C). A temperature reading gun can be extremely helpful, especially for measuring the temperature of the basking spot and taking the surface temperatures of pieces of decor in their habitat. During the night, do not let the tank drop below 65°F (18°C), or your gecko's body temperature will drop too much.

If you find the tank is dropping below 70°F (21°C), it would be best to purchase a heating pad or heat mat with an inbuilt thermostat. Heating pads and basking lights can be hooked up to a timer that automatically turns the heating equipment off/on at the appropriate times. Manufacturers make timer devices like this that are specific to reptile care, and they can be purchased at exotic pet stores. A slightly cheaper option could be purchasing one from a home improvement store, as many people use them for outdoor decorations for their homes or to turn lights on inside their homes automatically at a certain time.

Heat and Lighting Choices

During the day, make sure the temperature does not exceed 90°F (32°C) directly under the light where your leopard gecko sits. If the temperature goes above this, it can cause burns and discomfort. Even though the previously discussed lamp is for heating, it is best to keep the light off at night to mimic the natural cycle of day and night. This maintains the gecko's natural internal clock (circadian rhythm) because day (light) and night (darkness) intervals are provided. Timers can be helpful so the light can be shut off automatically, but geckos still need heat overnight. There are some bulbs made that emit red light or purple light to provide heat without the presence of too much bright light. Heat pads are also a great alternative to lamps.

UVB (ultraviolet B) bulbs are used with many species of reptiles to recreate the natural UV rays emitted by the sun. Leopard geckos are nocturnal, so most experts do not think they need UVB lights, but some people disagree and believe that a 2–5% UVB bulb will allow these lizards to make some vitamin D and store and use calcium. It is best to ask your vet, but if you decide to use one, make sure it is low-wattage because geckos can get sunburned or develop skin cancer in the presence of excessive UV rays.

When using any light bulbs, always have a spare bulb on hand for when the previous one burns out. You do not want to have to make a dash to the store or have a problem overnight.

Humidity

> *Some form of slight humidity should be given. This could be a daily misting of a live plant in the terrarium, using dampened moss under the animal's warm hide, or using a specific humidity hide.*
>
> STEPHANIE DILLON
> *Granite State Geckos*

Humidity is important, but misting the entire tank is unnecessary and may even cause problems. With some species of tropical geckos, this needs to be done daily, but leopard geckos come from a more arid environment, so they do not require or enjoy high humidity levels.

However, despite their dry habitat, they need a "humid spot" to ensure their respiratory and shedding systems are healthy. Leopard geckos shed more frequently than most lizards. It is thought that they do this in the wild to reduce their scent and thereby decrease the likelihood that predators will detect them.

In their natural habitat, these geckos will burrow and seek moisture and cool environments when they need them. This is most often when they are shedding, as moisture prevents stuck shed. If shedding does not proceed normally and skin gets stuck on their tails or toes, the circulation may be cut off, and the affected body part may be lost. It is part of your responsibility to watch out for stuck shed. The best way to replicate this humid spot in a domestic setting is by misting live plants, using dampened moss, or – and this is by far the best option – by using "humid hides."

HEALTH ALERT
Healthy vs. Unhealthy

A healthy leopard gecko will have clear eyes, a slightly fatty belly, and shed completely. Check around fingers, eyes, and nose for retained shed. On the other hand, an unhealthy leopard gecko will have a poor appetite, bent limbs, and/or sunken eyes.

Photo Courtesy of Lynn Rodrigues

These hides should be placed on the warm side of the habitat. You could make one out of a small box, coconut shell, reptile cave, or some other type of smallish enclosed or semi-enclosed shelter into which you have put hydrophilic substrate. Hydrophilic substrate absorbs water, and some examples are coconut coir, peat moss, or eco-earth. In a pinch, moist paper towels do the trick! Then, mist the humid hide until it is moist and check it regularly to ensure it does not dry out, and neither does your gecko's skin. Keeping the humid hide moist should be part of your weekly routine.

In summary:

- These lizards use their environment to control or regulate their body temperature.
- You need to provide a habitat that offers a range of temperatures within it.
- The warm end should be kept at 86–98F (30–37°C).
- A heat lamp or mat creates the warm area the gecko will use for basking and at night. The lamp should be switched off at night.
- The opposite end of the tank must be cooler at around 75–79°F (24–26°C).
- These geckos do not enjoy a humid environment, so this should be controlled at 30 to 40%. It is best to measure the tank humidity at the cool end.

This may sound overwhelming, but once the tank is set up and you get into the routine of measuring temperature, etc., you will realize it is a very small price to pay for the joy of having a leopard gecko!

At-a-Glance Fact Sheet

- Leopard geckos do not like high temperatures and prefer to hide in the shade during the hottest parts of the day.
- These lizards are ectothermic/cold-blooded, and their body temperature is determined by that of the air around them.
- Providing a constant temperature gradient within the tank so that the gecko can adjust its own temperature is crucial.
- Monitor temperatures with one (or two) accurate thermometers.
- Use a heating pad or heat mat with an inbuilt thermostat if the tank temperature drops too low, especially at night.
- The lamp is for heating but should be off at night to mimic the natural cycle of day and night.
- These geckos do not require or enjoy high humidity levels, but they need a humid hide to ensure their respiratory and shedding systems are healthy.
- You can make your own humid hide.
- Keeping the humid hide moist should be part of your weekly routine.

CHAPTER 8

Food and Water

> *During winter months, some leopard geckos' appetites and activity levels will decrease. This is called brumation, and while not all leopard geckos will experience this, it is completely normal for them to go into a more dormant state in their natural environment. Don't stress, and keep providing access to food and water while monitoring that the gecko is maintaining a healthy weight. Leopard geckos can go weeks and even months without food, as they should have a reserve built up in their tails for occasions like this.*
>
> MARK BRUNSDON
> *CAN Geckos*

As with any pet, ensuring that your leopard gecko has the ideal diet is essential. It is necessary to understand the foods available to you, how often to feed your pet, how to identify why it is not eating, and how to use supplements to further boost the health of your lizard.

Food

Leopard geckos feed primarily on live, moving insect prey. An appropriate diet may consist of commercially raised crickets with supplemental additions of silkworms, roaches, grasshoppers, mealworms, dubia roaches, superworms, waxworms, fruit flies, soldier fly larvae,

Chapter 8: Food and Water

Photo Courtesy of Christina Hulett

moths, and other live insects. Do not feed mealworms or superworms to geckos that are younger than eight months, however. They cannot digest them properly, and their digestive systems may become impacted, a potentially fatal condition.

While variety is ideal, mealworms or crickets are considered a staple diet for these geckos. A warning about crickets, though: they can give a painful stab with their leg spikes and are escape artists. Do not leave crickets unattended in the tank to make sure they (a) stay in the tank and (b) get eaten by your gecko. If your pet shows no interest in the cricket or some of them, remove them from the tank.

Individual geckos may prefer some foods over others, just like we each have our own favorite foods. A varied diet that requires a range of hunting skills is also a good idea for both nutrition and activity. Ultimately, offering a variety can make for happier, healthier geckos. It is great to start them on a varied diet when they are young so they do not become fussy eaters as adults. Also, each different food source provides different nutrients.

Using some live food that your gecko must chase will provide awesome stimulation and exercise for your pet and is a great way to simulate natural hunting conditions. It is a lot more engaging for your pet than just eating out of a bowl or tray. A further option is to move feeder insects around the tank so they are not always in the same place. Again, this stimulates the gecko to hunt.

An important word of caution, though. Do not feed your pet insects that you catch in your home, yard, or neighborhood. They may be contaminated with pesticides or herbicides or even carry parasites. Tempting as it is to avoid the costs and effort of buying foods, it is important to acquire them from a reputable source that will not sell you food that may pose a health hazard to your gecko.

Baby leopard geckos should be fed five to seven small crickets or mealworms every day until they reach about four inches long. Baby geckos need the nutrients to grow and become strong. Larger food should be offered to them every other day until they become full-grown adults at about 10 to 12 months old. Juveniles should be fed every one to two days, and adults should be fed two to three times per week.

Some adult geckos will enjoy the added nutrients of a pinky or infant mouse. Just make sure the mouse is not too big; going smaller is always better if you are unsure. To keep its natural feeding and hunting rhythms, try to feed your gecko at dusk or dawn.

The following table provides a broad overview of what to feed your gecko at various ages and at what frequency:

Age	Food	Frequency
Babies	5-7 small crickets	Daily
	Larger food like roaches, moths, black soldier fly larvae, waxworms, silkworms, dubia roaches, and grasshoppers	Occasionally (1 item)
Juveniles	10-15 medium crickets	Every 1-2 days
	Larger food like superworms, mealworms, roaches, moths, black soldier fly larvae, waxworms, silkworms, dubia roaches, and grasshoppers	Every 2-3 days (1 item)
Adults	10-15 large crickets	2-3 times per week
	Larger food like pinky (infant) mice, superworms, mealworms, roaches, moths, black soldier fly larvae, waxworms, silkworms, dubia roaches, and grasshoppers	Every 3-4 days (1 item)

One way to make sure your gecko is provided with the best nutrients from its food is to gut-load insects and dust them. Gut loading is feeding the live insects a varied and healthy diet before you feed them to your gecko. This can be done using fruits and vegetables or by purchasing a supplement specifically designed for this. Fluker's makes a great one, but you can ask your vet or the staff at an exotic pet store for advice. You could also dust the insects with a vitamin supplement suggested

Photo Courtesy of Chelsea O'Brien

for leopard geckos. There are many supplements available from many different manufacturers.

It is important that you take care of your feeder insects. Ensure they eat and drink to keep them alive and so they provide optimum nutrition to your leopard gecko. For example, mealworms are kept in the fridge, but they need to be taken out every 24 hours to eat and drink, and silkworms need plentiful, clean, and fresh leaves to feed on.

Dead insects are another food option, often preferred by squeamish pet owners, who would rather not buy or handle live bugs. Despite the convenience, using dead food is not recommended for several reasons. Firstly, dead crickets have little to no moisture, which can lead to a dehydrated gecko. Secondly, they have little nutritional value. In addition, and worryingly, they can attract parasites and bacteria that could be harmful to your gecko's health. Finally, they prevent geckos from going through the natural act of hunting, which is a negative both physically and emotionally. Often, geckos will reject dried insects as they do not move, and movement is what triggers their predation response, encouraging them to eat.

It may be tempting to share your snacks with your gecko, and some fruits have nutritional value to them, but most vets will advise you not to provide them. In the wild, geckos will not eat anything except live insects. Offering a little piece of fruit or vegetable may potentially cause real damage to your pet because geckos cannot digest cellulose (plant material). This, too, can lead to impaction.

It can be alarming to first-time gecko owners when their geckos do not eat, but many adult geckos can go without food for 10 days to two weeks due to the fat storage in their tails. Unlike mammals, reptiles generally eat less and do not require very much food to survive. It is not even unusual for healthy, adult geckos to only eat once a month.

In addition, geckos go into a more dormant state, called brumation, during the winter months. This period of decreased appetite and activity is entirely normal and not a cause for worry. Not all geckos experience this change, though. Either way, continue to provide your pet with food and water. The sign to look out for that will alert you to the fact that your gecko is not in a dormant state but unwell is a noticeable loss of weight and condition.

The second annual period when healthy geckos may stop eating is in the breeding season. There are no set seasons or months for this. If you have a female gecko, she may not eat while her body gets ready to lay eggs. This is entirely normal, too, and no cause for concern unless she starts to look sick.

HELPFUL TIP
Mouse or Not?

A leopard gecko's diet should be composed primarily of insects, including crickets, mealworms, and waxworms. But can your leopard gecko eat mice? While an adult mouse is too large for a leopard gecko's meal, a pinkie or baby mouse is an appropriate occasional treat. Mice are too fatty for a daily diet staple but can benefit your gecko in small amounts.

> *The best nutritional advice I could give would be to take care of your feeder insects! They need to eat and drink to stay alive and be a healthy food source for your leopard gecko! Folks don't often think about this, especially in regard to mealworms that you generally keep refrigerated. It's very important to take those guys out of the fridge at least once a week for at least 24 hours so they can eat and drink.*
>
> STEPHANIE DILLON
> *Granite State Geckos*

However, your gecko's poor appetite could be a result of other factors which should be addressed as soon as you are aware of them:

- Overhandling: this can cause your gecko to become very stressed and stop eating as a result. You will get to know what is okay and what is too much.
- Conditions in the tank, such as lighting or temperature, that are not correct may also cause stress, so it is smart to check the lighting, temperature, and humidity to eliminate or identify them as the problem.
- A further possibility is that there is too much activity near or around the tank. A great deal of movement or an overly curious dog or cat may also stress your gecko.
- If the lack of appetite is accompanied by other symptoms, such as diarrhea or dramatic weight loss, the gecko may have a parasite infestation.
- Like people, some geckos are shy and prefer not to be watched when they hunt and eat; give them a little mealtime privacy.
- Your pet may not like the feed type you have opted for. Try some others and get to know what they enjoy and what they will not eat.
- Older geckos have less appetite than younger ones. Again, individuals vary. Some older pets may want to eat a couple of times a week, and others only show interest in food monthly. Do not ever try and get your gecko to eat more than it wants.

If the problem is caused by environmental issues in or around the habitat, take steps to remedy them as quickly as you can. Concerns around your gecko's health should be addressed to your vet. If you have an older gecko that is hunting and eating less, keep an eye on it and maintain its nutrition.

Lizards that are not eating as often will benefit from high-protein insects, such as superworms and dubia roaches, when they do eat. It is also important to provide multivitamins and calcium.

Supplements

> *While giving your gecko a variety of insect options is important in providing a well-balanced diet, it is absolutely critical that you also provide the appropriate vitamin supplementation. Your gecko will need access to a variety of vitamins that it will not otherwise get in a captive environment. You should be giving your gecko access to calcium with vitamin D3, as well as a multivitamin. A capful of supplementation should always be available in the gecko's enclosure.*
>
> MARK BRUNSDON
> *CAN Geckos*

In addition to a variety of (preferably live) insects, it is important that you provide – as part of a well-balanced diet – vitamin supplements. Although geckos usually get the vitamins they need when they are in the wild, owners must provide them to pets. There are three that are vital: calcium with vitamin D3, calcium, and a multivitamin formulated specifically for these critters. If you are unsure which of the options available is best or most suitable, ask a specialist or vet for advice.

Regardless of the type or brand of supplement you use, there should always be a capful of calcium *without* D3 in a suitable container in the tank. It is also important to remember that calcium and vitamins must

Photo Courtesy of Tiffany Sharpeta

be provided throughout the life of your gecko to keep it healthy and its bones strong. They enjoy licking at both calcium and multivitamins, so they will find them and ingest them.

To further bolster their intake, you can dust your feeders with calcium *with* D3 and with multivitamins two or three times a week. The required supplements are:

- Calcium with D3
- Calcium without D3 or phosphorous
- Reptile multivitamin
- Gut-loaded feeder insects

Water

Geckos need a shallow water tray in their tanks, preferably made from inert, natural materials like rock, porcelain, or thick glass. Plastic can work, but the heat from the bulbs and mats may cause the plastic to warm up and leach chemicals into the water, which your pet will then be exposed to. The water bowl needs to be large enough for the gecko to climb into and soak, as this helps with healthy shedding. It should also be easily accessible for the gecko to lap the water up; they drink water in a comparable way to cats!

The water in the bowl should be changed at least every other day, but daily would be best. It can also be a good idea to put a large rock in the gecko's water. When you put crickets into the tank, they go to take a drink and slip into the bowl. They are unable to escape from the edges of the bowl, so a rock or piece of decor placed inside can be their escape route. Without this escape, the crickets die, and the water quality goes south very quickly. The dead crickets combined with the heat in the tank can make a very stinky soup if it is not cleaned quickly.

Some people use water bottles, and others use tap water. However, bottled water is the safest option. If you have well water, this is fine to drink. If you use city water provided by the state, it may contain chlorine, so water conditioners are recommended to remove the chemicals and additives in the water. These products can be found in any pet store that sells fish.

Regardless of what kind of container you select, remember to place the water dish or tray away from the basking lamp and in the cool end to prevent water loss and an increase in the overall humidity levels in the tank.

> *Leopard geckos can easily live to be 10 to 13 years old, and it really isn't uncommon for them to live to be 20 years old! They are generally very durable animals. Making sure your older gecko is coming out to drink water or lick the moisture off the cage is really important, as dehydration risk increases with age. Having multiple water dishes and frequent misting helps this.*
>
> TWYLA GROSS
> *Dakota Geckos*

At-a-Glance Fact Sheet

- Leopard geckos feed primarily on live, moving insect prey.
- A varied diet of live food requires a range of hunting skills, which is ideal for nutrition, stimulus, and exercise.
- Do not feed your pet insects caught in your home, yard, or neighborhood, as they may be contaminated.
- Babies and adults have different needs in terms of food types and feeding frequency.
- Ensure your gecko is provided with the best nutrients by gut-loading and dusting feeder insects with vitamin supplements.
- Using dead food is not recommended as they often contain little to no moisture, have little nutritional value, can attract parasites and bacteria, and they prevent geckos from going through the natural act of hunting.

At-a-Glance Fact Sheet ...Continued

- Fruit and vegetables may cause harm because geckos cannot digest cellulose.
- Adult geckos can go without food for 10 – 14 days due to the fat storage in their tails.
- Geckos go into a dormant state during the winter months when appetite and activity decrease.
- Healthy female geckos may stop eating in the breeding season.
- Other reasons for poor appetite could be a result of overhandling, tank conditions, stress, the gecko may not like the feed type on offer, or it may be ill.
- Leopard Geckos require calcium with D3, calcium without D3 or phosphorous, a reptile-specific multivitamin, and gut-loaded feeder insects.
- Geckos need a shallow water tray that is large enough for them to climb into and soak in, as this helps with healthy shedding.
- Water trays or bowls must be easily accessible for the gecko to lap from, and the water should be changed daily or at least every other day.
- The water dish or tray should be placed in the cool end to prevent water loss and an increase in the tank's overall humidity levels.

CHAPTER 9

Health and Wellness

The best way to care for your gecko is to be observant and to stay vigilant because you are your gecko's best health advocate. Reptiles are known to put up with and hide pain and distress, especially initially, so you need to be able to read the signs. As you get to know your gecko's personality, you will be able to tell when it is not acting like itself. Your lizard will display certain signs when it is doing well and when it is not.

Chapter 9: Health and Wellness

A healthy and contented leopard gecko will be bright and alert, hunting and eating well, moving with ease, spending time in both the warm and cool zones to regulate its body temperature, responding to movements, reacting to touch, and exploring its tank.

A loss of appetite (outside of the circumstances discussed in the previous chapter), lethargy, keeping its eyes closed (even when it is not asleep), tail waving, and jerky movements are signs that your lizard is either stressed or sick or both.

Be Vigilant

> *In the first few weeks of ownership, you should make sure that your gecko is defecating normally. Checking for stool and even providing your vet with a stool sample to perform a fecal exam is a good idea. Make sure it's also eating, even though this may not happen for a little while as it gets used to its new environment.*
>
> SEAN BERGMAN
> *E-ville Geckos*

It is essential to catch any health and well-being issues early. To identify problems, handle your gecko often, engage with it, and observe its behavior and body closely. This gives you the opportunity to know what is normal for your gecko and spot any potential issues that may be starting to arise. Identifying a problem early means you can have it seen by a vet or expert, such as a breeder, before it gets too serious. Vigilance goes together with maintaining feeding and cleaning routines and schedules.

But what if you're away from your gecko? It can be nerve-wracking to leave your pets when you go on vacation. With leopard geckos, it is usually okay to leave them alone for one to two days if they are on an established and correct food and water schedule. If you must leave your gecko for more than two days, I suggest having someone you trust and

Photo Courtesy of Nikki-Taylor Olivier

who is familiar with reptiles and their care come to check on it.

It is advisable to leave a checklist for any pet sitter, so they can easily ensure everything is done and adequately maintained. Below is a sample provided for you to use when you go on your next trip. The feeding days can vary depending on whether your gecko is a baby, juvenile, or adult. Please reference the previous chapter for feeding suggestions. It is also a good idea to meet your sitter beforehand and share all the gecko's requirements and your expectations when they care for your pet.

This example or sample outline is for an adult leopard gecko.

Name: A. Gecko Owner
Dates Traveling: 12/15/2023 - 12/26/23.
Dates to come and check on my gecko: 12/17/2023, 12/19/2023, 12/21/2023, 12/23/2023, 12/25/2023.
Number of visits per scheduled day: 1
My phone number: 123 456 7890
Emergency contact: Paul Smith, 098 765 4321, Chester, NJ
Exotic vet: Address: 123 Willow Avenue, Chester, NJ 07840
Phone number: 122 334 4556

Chapter 9: Health and Wellness

Please follow these instructions when caring for my leopard gecko

 Wash the water bowl with soapy water and rinse thoroughly.

 Refill the water bowl with water (bottled, tap, a jug placed by the tank, etc.).

 Provide supplements on 12/21/2023 by placing them in the tank for the gecko to lick.

 Feed 10 to 15 large crickets on 12/21/2023 and on 12/25/2023.

 Feed hornworm (or other supplemental food) on 12/19/2023 and 12/23/2023 and dampen paper towels for crickets.

 Check that all light bulbs and heat pads are working. Extra light bulbs are provided if you need them.

 Check the temperature in the tank on the hot side, where it should read about 90°F, and the cool side, which needs to be between 75 and 80°F. Please call me for instructions if the tank drops below 65°F!

 Spot-clean poop from the tank using tissue and dispose of it in the garbage.

 Please send me a photo and video of my gecko when you visit it.

I have placed all the supplements you will need to use next to the tank with instructions. The live crickets are in a plastic tank, so you can access them easily.

In addition to the above, or something like it, do the following for your gecko sitter:

- Leave written instructions next to, or written on, each supplement container.
- Do not forget to feed the crickets before you leave. They also need water, so place a damp paper towel or sponge in with them to drink from.
- Place any equipment or items you think the pet sitter may need, such as spare light bulbs, next to the tank so they can be found easily.
- Provide a water bottle in case your home loses power; it can be filled with hot water to keep your gecko warm in this type of emergency.
- Keep tissues and a trash can with a lid near your gecko tank so your sitter knows where to dispose of waste properly.

You may elect to provide additional instructions or items for your pet sitter. Ideally, get the sitter around to meet you and your gecko and be shown everything before you go away.

Keep Them Active

> *You should not have the gecko out for more than 15 minutes at a time, as they do get cold quickly due to their small size. Letting the gecko explore a safe space under supervision is great for its emotional well-being. I have a mini playpen meant for puppies I let my gecko explore in. The playpen has a large variety of hides, branches, and other textures. Adding a fold reward or hunting opportunities during playtime will help the gecko associate coming out of the cage with a reward.*
>
> TWYLA GROSS
Dakota Geckos

Exercise or activity is critical to your gecko's health. Not surprisingly, domestic leopard geckos move around less than wild ones do. Just as with humans, a balanced diet combined with exercise contributes significantly to a gecko's well-being and longevity. An enclosure large enough for exploration is vital to a healthy pet, and providing many surfaces to climb and explore can encourage your gecko to move around more. It is also fun to change up the decor in the enclosure occasionally to give your gecko a space that feels fresh and new, as this encourages exploration.

Sometimes it is hard to imagine reptiles feeling emotions because they do not change their facial expressions much, but they do appear to feel some emotions like ours. However, they still possess natural instincts that can cause them to respond defensively. Remember that if your gecko has a bad day, it does not mean it hates you!

Additional soaking can keep your gecko active. It can be helpful to soak your gecko in shallow warm water for 15 to 20 minutes about two to three times per week, and this is especially important while it is shedding to ensure all skin is removed.

Recognizing Health Problems

> *The biggest thing to be on the lookout for is the animal not eating or drinking and/or losing an excessive amount of weight quickly. If it isn't eating or drinking, this can be indicative of stress. Maybe the lights are too bright and are on too long, or the overall temperatures are not correct. Maybe there is another stressor, such as a curious cat or dog. However, if the animal is visibly losing excessive weight, this could indicate a parasitic infection, especially if accompanied by diarrhea.*
>
> STEPHANIE DILLON
> *Granite State Geckos*

As previously stated, lizards are good at looking healthy because, in the wild, a gecko that looks sick or weak is like a magnet for predators! Given you may not pick up problems early on because of this, it is a good idea – if your pet is willing and able to be handled – to weigh your gecko weekly and keep records. Some owners keep notes of shedding, feeding, and behavior. All of this can help you spot issues and can be a fantastic resource to show a reptile vet if you need to consult one.

When observing your pet, look for trouble breathing, difficulty moving, drooping head or limbs, gaping mouth, thinning tail, lethargy, vocalizing (which can indicate stress and/or pain), weakness, vomiting/regurgitation, weight loss, and loss of appetite. Be sure to contact your vet if you see any of these signs.

As discussed in the section on food and feeding, it is okay and normal for leopard geckos to go for a few days without eating, especially during the winter when they also may become sluggish, thanks to the colder weather. They live off the fat stored in their tail as their metabolism slows. Keep this in mind if your gecko eats less in the winter; just be sure it is not going for too long without a meal and is not losing body mass quickly.

Most Common Ailments

> *The most common issue with reptiles is metabolic bone disease, which presents as 'droopy' or weak limbs, jaw disfiguration, and general decline. This disease is progressive, so it will continue to get worse without calcium treatments. Like any pet, keeping an eye on feces is always a good indicator of health. Look out for green/yellow feces or extremely wet/dry feces. Yellow/green feces may indicate some sort of liver issue; geckos are known to have fatty liver disease. If these signs are presenting, it is best to take the animal to an exotic vet.*
>
> TWYLA GROSS
> *Dakota Geckos*

The most common ailments leopard geckos are prone to are intestinal impaction, parasitic infestation, malnutrition, metabolic bone disease (MBD)/nutritional secondary hyperparathyroidism, hypovitaminosis, dysecdysis, hemipene infections, abscesses, egg binding when breeding, respiratory infections, tail loss, stick tail disease, and bacterial dermatitis. You can learn to recognize these conditions.

1. **Intestinal impaction:** As referred to earlier, this condition is the number one cause of death and is due to the ingestion of something that cannot be digested or passed normally. Symptoms include appetite loss, weight loss, constipation, bloated belly, lethargy, and, in some cases, a dark blue spot that can be seen on the side of the belly. You can address the problem by giving your gecko a warm bath and very gently massaging its belly. Some pet owners also give a drop of mineral or olive oil orally. If the blockage persists, you must consult a vet!

2. **Parasites:** The most common types are pinworms and coccidia. They can be passed on by other lizards or poor-quality, contaminated

food. Signs of parasites in your gecko appear as regurgitation/vomiting, dramatic loss of weight, including thinning of the tail, loss of appetite, diarrhea, very smelly fecal matter, and lethargy. The only conclusive way to diagnose parasites and identify the type is through a stool test done by a vet. If the test confirms the diagnosis, a dewormer will be prescribed. Do not medicate your gecko or fail to follow instructions, as the incorrect dose can be fatal.

3. **Malnutrition:** This is a disease linked either to owner neglect (an inadequate or poor diet) or another medical condition. The condition manifests as lethargy, loss of appetite, a skinny tail, and weight loss. A vet will help you find out if you are dealing with malnutrition or parasites, as the symptoms are very similar.

4. **Metabolic Bone Disease** (MBD): This disease is caused by improper calcium and/or vitamin D3 availability or absorption, which results in soft bones. Common symptoms in leopard geckos are distorted limbs; stuck shed; anorexia; a reluctance to move; hard lumps along the spinal column, legs, or jaw; unusual jaw flexibility; and difficulty raising the body off the ground due to weak legs. This condition is also referred to as *nutritional secondary hyperparathyroidism*. It is 100% preventable – by you, the owner! Feed your gecko a diet that includes the vitamins and supplements it needs (see Chapter 7 for details). If your pet does not improve after a month of the correct supplements, see your vet.

5. **Hypovitaminosis:** This health problem is also the result of poor diet and inadequate supplement provision. In leopard geckos, the symptoms include dull skin color (not to be confused with the start of shedding), decreased appetite, trouble hunting/catching food, squinting eyes, excess tear production, shedding problems, and retained hemipenal casts or plugs. Again, this condition can be avoided by providing correct feeding and care.

6. **Dysecdysis:** When a gecko is unable to shed fully and normally, sections of retained sheds build up around the toes or tail. They begin to restrict blood flow, and the affected tissue begins to die. This presents itself in geckos by causing pale skin, the loss of toes

or the tail, appetite loss, and closed or squinting eyes. You can avoid this by maintaining a moist or damp hide to prevent the skin from becoming too dry. If your pet is struggling to shed, you can help by soaking the stuck skin and then removing it very gently with a damp paper towel.

7. **Hemipene infections:** The hemipene is the bi-lobed male reproductive organ that is tucked beneath the tail, normally emerging from the body during mating. If the hemipene becomes infected, one or two pink bulges will appear under the male's cloaca caused by the swelling and infection of the penis. Consult a vet or reptile specialist; severe infections will require antibiotics.

8. **Abscesses:** Unfortunately, these lizards are prone to abscesses under the skin, including around the eyes. These appear as lumps or bumps under the skin that are not equivalent on both sides. They can also be present inside the mouth. A vet will drain the abscess, clean it out, and provide antibiotics and painkillers for you to give your pet.

9. **Egg binding:** This naturally only occurs in female leopard geckos. These lizards lay eggs in pairs, so if only one egg is laid, you need to investigate. The symptoms of a retained or bound egg include hard lumps in the abdomen, lethargy, possible tissue protrusion from the cloaca, and a strained or swollen cloaca. A vet may perform a scan, and the egg will be removed.

10. **Respiratory infections:** These chest/lung infections are bacterial in nature and

HEALTH ALERT
Identifying Intestinal Impactions

Intestinal impactions are more common for geckos who live on sand, fine gravel, or crushed walnut shell substrate. Dehydration, parasites, and overfeeding can also cause impaction. Signs of this condition include:
- Lethargy
- Lack of appetite
- Straining to defecate
- Decreased stool output

Prevention is the best action for intestinal impaction, but treatment is possible if identified quickly. Untreated intestinal impaction can lead to complete organ failure and death.

Photo Courtesy of Amy Sisco

the result of poor temperature and/or humidity control in the tank. Symptoms of this type of infection include difficulty breathing, which may manifest as breathing through the mouth, loss of appetite, clogged nostrils, bubbly saliva, and lethargy. A visit to the vet will confirm the diagnosis, and the appropriate treatment, including antibiotics and probiotics, can be given. Additional hydration may also be required during recovery.

11. ***Stick Tail Disease:*** This is something of a misnomer in that this is not a discreet condition or illness but an extremely serious symptom of a range of health problems. Stick tail disease is a blanket term for rapid and severe weight loss that reduces the normally fat tail to skin and bone. It is usually accompanied by other symptoms such as lethargy, diarrhea, loss of appetite, and going into hiding. This alarming condition can be caused by severe stress, temperatures that are too low, vitamin deficiency, parasite infestation, or

an internal abscess. This type of quick and dramatic weight loss should ring loud alarm bells, and you need to take your gecko to the vet. Once there, fecal and blood samples will be taken, and an examination done to identify the underlying cause and treat it.

12. **Bacterial Dermatitis:** This is an extensive bacterial skin infection that, if untreated, can become really nasty. These infections are usually the result of incorrect tank conditions or nutrition, inadequate care, poor hygiene, or following an injury. Early symptoms are usually small, red wounds or blister-like sores on the skin. These can become larger or rupture and turn into far larger and deeper wounds. This illness must be treated by a vet, and it is essential to identify why it arose in the first place!

DID YOU KNOW?
Calcium Stores

Leopard geckos need calcium supplements to stay healthy and survive, but they can store their calcium in a unique place. If you look carefully at a leopard gecko, you may be able to see two small lumps under its armpits. These lumps are called "armpit bubbles" and contain vitamins, protein, minerals, and calcium. These bubbles are completely normal but can also sometimes indicate a weight problem.

As indicated, you can avoid many of these by feeding your gecko correctly, ensuring tank temperature and humidity are correct, and keeping the habitat clean. You can address some of them yourself, such as stuck shed and tail loss. However, sometimes you must seek help from a specialist vet. There are several symptoms that should sound loud alarms for you and lead to a trip to the vet:

- Thinning tail
- Gaping mouth
- Breathing difficulty
- Discharge from the nose or eyes
- Lumps and swellings
- Lethargy and weakness
- Drooping limbs or head
- Weight loss
- Loss of condition
- Vomiting
- Prolapses from the cloaca.

Of course, if you notice anything about your leopard gecko that is not on this list that worries or concerns you, you can always consult a breeder, exotic pet store employee or owner, or another lizard owner you trust.

Shedding and Tail Dropping

> *One thing that a new owner should actively watch for is a stuck shed, and they should provide assistance with removal if it is observed. A stuck shed can impact blood flow to the affected regions and can ultimately result in the loss of toes or limbs if left untreated. There are many different ways to assist your gecko with releasing a stuck shed, but simply dampening the affected area and lightly rubbing the shed with a wet cotton swab will often release it.*
>
> MARK BRUNSDON
> *CAN Geckos*

Shedding is both necessary and natural for reptiles. Mostly it proceeds normally, and your gecko can handle it without your intervention. When your leopard gecko starts shedding, there are some clues before the skin falls off. Your gecko may appear dull in color, and occasionally, the old skin will separate from the gecko's body and remain intact, almost as if the reptile is wearing a poncho. Your gecko will eventually use its mouth to pull the skin off its body and will then eat it, which is entirely normal.

However, if you notice your gecko is having trouble removing the skin, you can soak the reptile in warm, shallow water up to its elbows. Let it soak for 10 to 15 minutes, then return it to the enclosure to finish the job. If it fails again, soak again, and use a damp washcloth to gently rub and remove excess skin from difficult areas like the toes. If the stuck skin is in a sensitive area like the eyes or cloaca and you are uncomfortable assisting, please consult your veterinarian.

Chapter 9: Health and Wellness

Photo Courtesy of Ashley Bryant

You can purchase products that ease the shedding process if your gecko is prone to difficulties. They can be purchased online or in pet stores or recommended to you by your breeder or vet. Look for areas like the toes, tail tip, cloaca, and eyes. These can quickly become problem areas. It is also common for leopard geckos to become a little shy, lethargic, and sometimes grumpy during their shed. They are more vulnerable during this stage and may retreat to the safety of their hides more often, especially their humid hide, which will ease the process for them.

One of leopard geckos' best self-defense options is losing or "dropping" their tails. When geckos do this, the tail wiggles on its own on the ground. In the wild, this will draw a predator to the discarded tail rather than the gecko itself, allowing it to run away safely. It can be alarming

Mediteranian Gecko with a recently dropped tail

to witness for first-time gecko owners, but it is normal. Gecko tails are perforated to allow them to fall off easily without losing blood or causing the formation of scar tissue. This can happen during handling or randomly while a gecko is alone in the tank. If this happens to your gecko, you can pick the discarded tail up with a tissue and dispose of it properly in the trash can.

If a tail is dropped, it will never grow back to its full length with a smooth taper to the tip, but it will grow back with a rounded or "nub-like" end. The regrowth will occur within 30 days of the initial drop. It does come at a cost, as the gecko is losing stored energy from fat in the tail, but it does not harm the reptile. Although tail loss is not uncommon, you need to safeguard your gecko's well-being until the new tail grows. Ensure that the tank conditions remain optimal and increase the amount of fatty food in the diet (such as waxworms or butter worms), as your pet's fat reserves were lost along with the tail. If you notice any sign of infection in the stump, consult your vet.

Chapter 9: Health and Wellness

At-a-Glance Fact Sheet

- You must become familiar with your leopard gecko's body and behavior and watch for any signs that something is not right so you can catch problems early.
- Your pet should be bright and alert, hunting and eating well, moving with ease, spending time in both the warm and cool zones to regulate its body temperature, responding to movements, reacting to touch, and exploring its tank.
- A loss of appetite, lethargy, keeping its eyes closed even when it is not asleep, tail waving, and jerky movements are signs that your lizard is either stressed or sick or both.
- Find a pet sitter if you will be away and leave a checklist and any equipment or items you think they may need next to the tank so they can be found easily.
- Weigh your gecko weekly and keep records of weight, shedding, feeding, and behavior.
- The most common ailments are intestinal impaction, parasitic infestation, malnutrition, metabolic bone disease (MBD)/nutritional secondary hyperparathyroidism, hypovitaminosis, dysecdysis, hemipene infections, abscesses, egg binding when breeding, respiratory infections, tail loss, stick tail disease, and bacterial dermatitis.
- You can avoid many of these by feeding your gecko correctly, ensuring tank temperature and humidity are correct, and keeping the habitat clean.
- Shedding is both necessary and natural for reptiles, but if it does not proceed normally, intervene to prevent health problems.
- Tail loss is not uncommon, but you need to safeguard your gecko's well-being until the new tail grows, as it has lost the fat reserves contained in its tail.

CHAPTER 10

Handling Tips

Geckos are like people in that they each have their unique personalities and preferences. When handling your gecko, do not force the interaction. It is always better to be patient, especially in the beginning. By forcing interaction, you are starting your relationship with your gecko off on the wrong foot, and it will quickly learn to distrust you.

All Geckos Are Different

> *I recommend not overhandling. It's important not to stress out your leopard gecko because this can cause it to stop eating in some cases. Every leopard gecko is different, so it's up to you to judge how much handling is too much for it.*
>
> SEAN BERGMAN
> *E-ville Geckos*

Younger geckos can be a bit fragile and require a delicate touch, but with adults, some enjoy handling more than others. By starting your handling routine with your gecko when it is young, there is a higher chance it will be more docile and calmer as it grows.

Keep this in mind when you decide where to purchase your gecko, as geckos purchased from breeders are typically more used to handling by humans. Starting your bonding process with a young leopard gecko yields better results.

Chapter 10: Handling Tips

Photo Courtesy of
Natalie Wittenbrook

Build Trust and Take It Slow

> *While it's generally uncommon, leopard geckos can and will bite! Notice the signs of aggravation, such as an arched back or the tail wagging high up and side to side. These are signs that it's time to give your gecko space!*
>
> STEPHANIE DILLON
> *Granite State Geckos*

It is tempting to start handling your gecko as soon as you get it but try to wait two weeks. Allowing your gecko time to settle in and adjust to its new home without handling will improve the chances of it being more relaxed and friendly.

By feeding the gecko, you are teaching it that you are the caregiver. Let the gecko get to know you by leaving your hand in the tank after feeding with the hope that your gecko will be curious and come to you eventually. Do not be scared if the gecko licks you; it is the reptile's way of exploring and learning about the world. It will also help the gecko get used to your smell. At this early stage, do not attempt to pick it up.

If your gecko eventually approaches you, gently rub or stroke its back to start with before you even try to pick it up. Keeping your gecko active and giving it attention is important but try not to overhandle it, especially early in your relationship. Too much right away can cause stress, which can ultimately cause health problems for the gecko.

Picking Up Your Leo

When picking up your gecko, start by placing your hand in the tank, palm up. Do not scoop up or lift your gecko immediately; let it get used to being in your hand. You can slowly slide your hand under its chin to give it some encouragement if needed. Once your gecko is on your palm, you can easily lift your hand and hold your gecko. They are curious creatures and will eventually climb onto your hand on their own. If your gecko is a bit skittish, that is okay. Give it time, and do not force it, or the gecko will lose trust in you. Patience is key! Also, do not hold your pet for too long initially. Pick it up, hold it for a few minutes (unless it starts to protest by squeaking, hissing, and/or wriggling), and then put it back down. At this stage, your hand – with or without your gecko in it – should stay in the tank.

Even if your gecko is giving signals that it would like to interact with you and be handled, do not just put your hand into the tank and grab it. Adult geckos are sturdier than youngsters, but they should still be handled gently to avoid frightening or injuring them. These pets also prefer warm hands, so make sure you are not cold or cool, so your gecko enjoys lounging on your palm.

Conversely, there are signals that your pet does not want to be picked up or interacted with. If a gecko is wagging its tail high up and/or arching its back, it is warning you to leave it alone and give it space. It is rare, but a stressed leopard gecko will bite. Another sign that your pet needs a break is if it hides. Do not take it personally or force matters; just give your pet time and space.

There may be instances where it is necessary to pick your gecko up even if it is not keen, such as when it needs care. When you do, be sure to support its whole body and use as loose a grip as possible without it being open enough for your gecko to slip or fall. Never lift your gecko by its tail, as it will cause the reptile to drop it. After working with your gecko for a bit, slowly and patiently, it should allow you to pick it up comfortably. This is a good sign that your pet trusts you.

> *Handling should always occur in a safe setting, over a counter or close to the floor, and using the hand-over-hand method. Don't firmly grip them, as geckos generally dislike being restrained. When removing the gecko from the enclosure, you can place your hand directly in front of your pet and allow it to climb onto your hand themselves. Or you can scoop it up by placing your hand under the abdomen.*
>
> **STEPHANIE DILLON**
> *Granite State Geckos*

PICKING UP YOUR LEOPARD GECKO FOR THE FIRST TIME
A STEP-BY-STEP GUIDE

01 Look in the tank and see if your gecko is out of its hide and looking at you with interest.

02 Place your hand flat in the tank, with your palm upwards, in front of the gecko.

03 Be calm and confident as you let the gecko lick and look at your hand.

04 If the gecko does not step up immediately, gently urge it to do so by placing your hand under its chin.

05 If your gecko runs and hides, give it space and try again later.

06 Once your gecko steps onto your hand, loosely wrap your hand around your gecko to secure it from falling when you move your hand. Use two hands if it is easier.

07 Bring your gecko to the ground or a comfortable surface so it is not high up while you're interacting with it.

08 Allow your gecko to walk across your hand and offer the other hand under its chin so it can walk back and forth if it wants to do so.

09 Please do not overdo it; be sure to gradually lead up to spending lots of time with your gecko so it does not feel overwhelmed or stressed.

Chapter 10: Handling Tips

Advanced Tips

There are other factors and tips associated with handling your gecko that can make your interactions easier and more successful and strengthen your bond:

- It is typically not best to wake them during the day to play because it messes with their natural sleep rhythms. Geckos are more likely to be open to handling when they first wake up. Be sure to be visibly present near the tank so you do not startle your gecko, but do not be overbearing or loud. Hold yourself calmly and confidently because your gecko can sense if you are anxious.

- Remember, especially when you first start handling your gecko, to do so in a controlled environment. You do not want to restrain your gecko's movements, but you also do not want it to be able to get

Photo Courtesy of Lynn Rodrigues

into gaps under heavy furniture or other areas you cannot access. The balance you need to strike will allow you to gently handle your gecko so that it is comfortable and can move around your hands or elsewhere, such as your lap or arm.

- Hand feeding can be a great bonding exercise for you and your gecko to get comfortable with each other. This can allow your gecko to get used to your smell and to be pleased about – and excited by – the presence of your hand, as it knows you are bringing it food. Be very careful, though, as sometimes geckos do not have the best aim when launching at their food. It is good to work up to hand feeding by starting with longer feeding tongs and slowly shortening them over time. Eventually, once you feel your gecko can grab the food accurately, you can use your hands. Always remember there is a chance the gecko could miss its prey and accidentally bite you. Do not lose trust in your pet; it did not intentionally bite you.

Photo Courtesy of Meagan Hazelton

Chapter 10: Handling Tips

- While your leopard gecko is shedding, it may not want to interact with you. This could mean hiding from you when you approach or refusing to be held. Coming to the tank while it is feeding or checking on it may cause your gecko to feel stressed. Give your pet space and check on it from a distance when possible.

- Some signs of stress and over-handling are skittish or aggressive behavior when being handled, wagging the tail, breathing quickly, spending lots of time in the hide, or looking dull in color.

- You can do several bonding exercises with your gecko to slowly build its trust in you. One option is to sit on the floor with your gecko in one hand and slowly slide your other hand underneath its chin, urging it onto that hand. It should climb up and settle. Once settled, repeat these motions, and let your gecko climb.

- Another exercise you can do is to allow your gecko to walk across your lap, and once it reaches the edge, allow the reptile to step up onto your hand and then repeat this process. Repetitive, slow patterns like this and the one described above enable your gecko to predict your next move while having the option to explore. You will also get to know your gecko's behavior, and you can find safer ways to build your trust with it.

- If you have two people present, you can sit on the floor and press your feet against your friend's feet to create a barrier so your gecko cannot run away. Keep your legs flat on the ground, so there is no room for escape underneath them. Place your gecko on the floor

gently and allow it to walk back and forth from person to person. You can make this more fun for your gecko by offering snacks during this time. You can increase your pet's hunting skills by placing a worm somewhere in the enclosed area to allow the gecko to find it independently.

In addition to creating a bond between you and your gecko, giving your pet exercise and stimulation, and providing enjoyment to you, these activities also have another important benefit. As mentioned, you will get to know how your reptile looks, behaves, and moves when it is well and happy. This makes it more likely that you will quickly pick up when it is not well.

Kids

> *When establishing trust with your leopard gecko, using tongs to hand feed is a great way to build trust. Offering your gecko food via tongs is a great way to show your hand is not food or a threat. From there, you can begin to handle the gecko by carefully scooping it up and holding it close to your body. Never let your gecko free roam on the ground, and never let inexperienced handlers, including children, handle a leopard gecko without supervision.*
>
> DYLAN AND SAM JONES
> *Galactic Reptiles*

When children handle your leopard gecko, it is best to have clear rules. If a child scares the leopard gecko, that can cause the reptile to lose trust, and it can be challenging to heal the relationship. Worse, children may become excited and accidentally hurt or injure the gecko. Generally, small children should not handle young geckos as these reptiles are more fragile than adults, and very young children have little sense of their own relative strength. Pets can be "loved to death," which is tragic and affects the child negatively, too.

Therefore, it is essential to provide your children with a list of things they should and should not be doing. For example, they should not grab, rush, or overhandle the gecko. They should be calm, mindful, patient, and gentle. I suggest that you show the child or children how you interact with your pet so that they can do the same. It can also be helpful to set a schedule for children to only hold the

FUN FACT: Barking Lizards

Leopard geckos make a range of sounds to communicate, including clicking, barking, and chirping. When your lizard barks or chirps, it could be indicating hunger, stress, or fear. Male geckos may bark when feeling territorial or as part of a mating call.

Dos and Don'ts for Interacting with Your Leopard Gecko

Do

- Do think of safe ways to develop the bond between you and your gecko.
- Do give your gecko opportunities to explore new things and surfaces safely.
- Do be mindful and patient. If you come on too strong or scare your gecko, developing a trusting relationship with it can be challenging.
- Do allow children to interact, but ensure they are monitored and that clear rules are established for the gecko's safety.
- Do offer your pet occasional treats outside of the enclosure.
- Do make sure your gecko is not overly hungry when you try to handle it, as this can cause a prey response when you place your hand in the tank.
- Do make sure your gecko is not out of the tank long enough to get very cold.

Do not

- Do not grab your gecko; place your hand flat and allow it to walk onto it.
- Do not pick your gecko up by the tail.
- Do not touch the gecko's eyes or mouth unnecessarily.
- Refrain from overhandling your gecko; give it a day a two between handling to ensure it does not get stressed.
- Do not squeeze your gecko; wrap your hands around it loosely.
- Don't hold your gecko up high. If it falls from high up, it could be badly hurt. When holding your gecko, sit on the ground or sofa so if it falls off your hand, it does not fall far, and ensure it lands on something soft.
- Do not force your gecko to come out if it is hiding; it will look for you when it wants to interact.
- Do not handle your gecko too much when it is shedding.

Chapter 10: Handling Tips

Dos and Don'ts for Interacting with Your Leopard Gecko Continued...

Do

- Do make it a family event and allow your gecko to bond with everyone.
- Do keep other pets out of the room when your gecko is out of the enclosure.
- Do have fun discovering your gecko's personality!

Do not

- Do not handle your gecko directly after eating. This can cause it to regurgitate food.
- Do not be fearful or disappointed if your gecko is not keen on being handled at first; these bonds take time. Be patient and keep trying when the gecko feels up to it.

gecko once every few days. You could even use time with the leopard gecko as a reward for good behavior.

When you first get your gecko, give it two weeks of no handling (marked in red) so it can get used to its new home. From there, handle the gecko every few days by allowing it to get used to you and your hand. For both your and your gecko's sake, take the time to interact the right way. Then, enjoy spending time with and learning about your new pet!

By the second month of ownership, you can start to hold your gecko every other day but be sure to align this schedule with feeding. I recommend waiting one

MAY

M	T	W	T	F	S	S
	1	2	3	4	5	6
7	8	9	10	11	12	13
14	15	16	17	18	19	20
21	22	23	24	25	26	27
28	29	30	31			

to two days after feeding before allowing handling and exercise.

For both your and your gecko's sake, take the time to interact the right way. Then, enjoy spending time with and learning about your new pet!

JUNE

M	T	W	T	F	S	S
	1	2	3	4	5	6
7	8	9	10	11	12	13
14	15	16	17	18	19	20
21	22	23	24	25	26	27
28	29	30	31			

Photo Courtesy of Mikayla Sullivan

At-a-Glance Fact Sheet

- By starting your handling routine when your pet is young, there is a greater chance it will be more docile and calmer.
- Never force your lizard to interact with you!
- Let your gecko get to know you by leaving your hand in the tank after feeding.
- Do not be scared if the gecko licks you. It is the reptile's way of learning and will help it get used to your smell.
- When your pet approaches you, gently rub or stroke its back, and do not try to pick it up at first, as this builds trust.
- When picking up your gecko, start by placing your hand in the tank, palm up.
- Do not lift your hand until your gecko is used to being in your hand.
- If your lizard is wagging its tail high up and/or arching its back, give it space.
- Support your pet's whole body and use a loose grip without it being open enough for your gecko to slip or fall.
- When you first start handling your gecko, do so in a controlled environment.
- Hand feeding can be a great bonding exercise but start with longer feeding tongs and slowly shortening them before you can use your hands to avoid accidental nips.
- There are bonding exercises you can do.
- Children require clear rules and supervision when they handle your leopard gecko.

CHAPTER 11

Breeding

> *Leopard geckos are solitary animals; if you plan on getting more than one, they should be housed separately. They should not cohabitate. Even when it comes to our breeders, we only pair them up for short periods—maybe a day or two during breeding season—before separating them. Cohabitated leopard geckos can fight over food and resources, overbreed, or stress out one another. Reptiles don't do well with stress, and fighting/dominant behavior can result in dropped tails and other injuries to your animals.*
>
> PATRICK KAMBEROS
> *Cold Blooded and Bizarre*

Leopard Geckos are thought to be one of the easiest reptiles to breed. As with anything, though, success is not a sure thing, and problems can arise. Having a pair of these smiling lizards does not mean you must allow them to breed. So, think carefully and be sure it is something you want to take on.

If you decide you do want to breed these critters, this chapter will introduce you to the basics of how to determine the sex of the geckos, egg laying and incubation, and raising hatchlings. We will also go over what you will need, like the types of geckos, space to house them, egg boxes, incubation boxes, and housing for the hatchlings.

Chapter 11: Breeding

Choosing to Breed

Yes, leopard geckos may be easy to breed, but is it really what you want to do? Ask yourself if you, in all honesty, have the time, energy, and money to dedicate to keeping your adults healthy and caring for the eggs and the hatchlings. Breeding these lizards has implications for you and your pets, so it is not a decision to be taken automatically or lightly. There are reasons why breeding geckos might not be a great idea:

- If the female is not always in top physical condition, the demands of egg laying can take a heavy toll or even prove fatal due to complications such as egg binding.

Photo Courtesy of Dean Host Jr. Origami Geckos

- Even if your breeding female stays healthy, her life expectancy will be shorter than that of males and even non-breeding females.
- You also need to decide what you will do with the babies. Will you be able to find good new owners or reptile retailers to sell them to in your area? Shipping geckos is not easy and can be risky for young lizards as they may become stressed or even injured. It is not practical for you to keep them because of the number of babies each female can produce per breeding season. In addition, you will require additional equipment, space, and food, which costs money you may not have.
- If you have dreams of large-scale, profitable breeding, remember that you will have to learn all about genetics so you know which morphs to breed with or cross-breed with. Rolling the genetic dice without knowledge and understanding can have unexpected results. Acquiring the knowledge, your breeding pairs, space, and equipment takes a serious investment of time and financial resources. There are also ongoing overheads such as utilities, feed, consumables, and – potentially – vet costs.

Assuming you are still keen to breed your leopard geckos, you need to plan and prepare. The leopard gecko breeding season is long, and the proper setup is necessary if you want to participate.

Breeding

To start breeding leopard geckos, you must, of course, have a male and a female. You can increase your chances of successful mating by having more than one female available. However, rotating females is important because egg production and development require a lot of energy, and that can weaken your gecko over time. So, do not breed with the same female each time.

Before breeding your geckos, they should be at least one year old or weigh a minimum of 35 grams. Once they reach that point, they are sexually mature and ready to mate. Females will only lay one or two eggs per clutch or batch of eggs. However, they can have several clutches during the mating season.

It is not a good idea to keep multiple geckos in the same enclosure for an extended period. The female should be in a tank with a minimum size of 10 gallons, but more room than that is always better. There should be ample space and hides available for the geckos so they can have distance from each other if necessary.

You need to plan and prepare before you can embark on breeding these awesome little lizards:

- You need to select your breeding stock. Ideally, this should be a male and one or two females, all of which are 100% healthy and aged between 2 and 5 years old.
- Boost their health with extra food – dusted with a suitable multivitamin powder – and a wide variety of types of feeder insects. Some breeders always keep a dish of mealworms in the breeding pair's tank, and soldier fly larvae are great, as they are high in calcium.
- Ensure they get all the supplements they need to remain in optimal condition. Place calcium powder in the tank, too. These geckos instinctively know how much calcium they need to eat. Some breeders believe that you should give your breeding stock calcium with D3. The danger is that it is possible to overdose on D3.
- There are supplies and items of equipment that are necessary before breeding can begin:
  - A nesting or laying box with a moist substrate in it. Eco-earth and sphagnum moss are good options, and both must be kept moist.
  - An incubator, either a purchased one or a DIY improvisation, and an incubation medium such as vermiculite.
  - A lot of feeder insects, as your breeding pair will require extra food during the mating and egg-laying periods. While hatchlings and babies may eat less than adults, they require feeding more often.
  - Housing for the hatchlings, which includes suitable tanks or boxes, shelter, a substrate such as paper towels, and water trays.

So, yes, there is a lot you need to have and do if you are breeding these cute geckos. To counterbalance that is the fact that it is fascinating, and the hatchlings and young geckos are a delight!

Leopard geckos can be encouraged to breed any time of the year, but their regular wild breeding season is between January and September, which is summer. Females typically lay 6 to 16 eggs throughout a season in, as mentioned, clutches of two eggs each laying. Mating usually takes place at night, so you may not see it happen. It can be a rough encounter with the male biting the female on the back of the neck. One way to dial back any bullying is to house several females with one male, not the other way around. Males can breed with up to six females. Eggs are usually laid approximately 21 to 28 days after mating.

We looked at what you need to do before you start breeding these reptiles, but what about what not to do? Do not:

Do not

- Randomly select your breeding stock; it must be carefully chosen, as discussed.
- Leave a group of males and females together to let nature take its course. Geckos need to be ready to breed.
- Select geckos that are too young or too old. Underage females may mate but are unlikely to produce viable eggs.
- Breed with lizards that are not in peak physical condition and suffer from any genetic problems. Again, females that are not strong and healthy are less likely to lay viable eggs and normal clutches.
- Select morphs that are prone to health issues.
- Be too ambitious. Start with one or two females while you learn the ropes so that you do not become swamped by the demands and the number of hatchlings in your care.

Chapter 11: Breeding

Finally, it is time to introduce the breeding stock to each other. You can house breeding stock using the harem method, where one male and two or more females are placed in a tank together. This can help if you have a limited number of tanks and/or space. Alternatively, you can keep the male separately and then introduce a female to them. This method is more popular with more serious breeders who are using selective breeding and want and need to keep careful records of parents and offspring.

When male leopard geckos are placed into the tank, there should be excitement when they see the female. They often vocalize loudly initially and during mating, so do not be alarmed by hissing, chirping, or barking sounds. After putting them into the same tank, monitor them to ensure they are not reacting aggressively. Once reproduction is over, the male should be returned to his enclosure.

There are no special requirements for initiating breeding, but supporting the eggs can be more challenging and requires planning and preparation. On the other hand, hatchlings are easy to care for and do not even require any special food.

You also need to take extra care when including children in the process, as it can occasionally be graphic and even traumatic because adult geckos often hurt or eat their hatchlings. Be ready for the "nature talk" if you decide to involve your child or children. It can be heartbreaking when children anticipate a baby but are left in a "gecko-eat-gecko" world. Be prepared before you start, and be patient during the process.

Determining Sex

The first step in breeding is knowing the sex of your gecko or geckos. There are a few things to consider when determining if your gecko is male or female. It can be easier to identify males.

Male leopard geckos tend to be slightly more prominent and have pre-anal pores above the base of their tails. This can be easy to spot in an adult specimen: it looks like a line of dots forming a V shape at the base of the tail. Males also have two oval-shaped hemi penal bulges.

Special Care for Females

> *Once a year, female leopard geckos go through a breeding season that can start and end at varying times during the winter/spring months. During this time, a female leopard gecko may stop eating to prepare her body to lay eggs. Females don't have to be bred to develop infertile eggs, though this doesn't always occur.*
>
> **SEAN BERGMAN**
> *E-ville Geckos*

If your goal is to breed more than one female at a time, you will need a 20-gallon tank at a minimum. More space is required so that when the male is introduced, the geckos can get away from each other as they get to know one another.

In addition, make sure calcium supplements are available to the females and dust their feeder insects with supplements. Developing

Chapter 11: Breeding

eggs is draining for the females, and the extra calcium will help them stay healthy during egg development.

It is common for females to lose their appetite or stop eating during mating season, but the females may feed between ovulations or clutches and then begin eating normally again. The best thing to do is monitor them and provide ample food to replenish the fat stored in their tails when their appetite returns. The female's comfort and safety throughout reproduction are of the utmost importance.

The incubation temperature of gecko eggs determines the sex of the hatchling. Generally, female hatchlings are born after incubating at 80°F, while males are typically hatched at around 91°F. Eggs take 45 to 60 days to hatch, and hatchlings usually complete their first shed within 24 hours.

Egg Laying

In the wild, female leopard geckos lay their eggs under rocks or logs. When the eggs come out of the mother, they are not yet hardened and will take a while to develop their protective shell. The eggs are then incubated for roughly six to 10 weeks, depending on the environmental temperatures.

You will notice that your pregnant female will begin putting on weight, and if you gently hold her up or turn her over, you may be able to see the shape of the eggs through her skin. The gestation period varies from female to female but is usually 2 to 5 weeks. Laying signs to look out for in your female are restlessness and digging. She may also lose interest in food at this point, which is also normal. This indicates she is looking for a safe place to lay her eggs. All these behaviors mean you need to provide a nesting box in her tank.

You can easily make one out of items and materials you probably already have in your home. You will need a plastic container with a lid to make an egg box. The lid is important as it helps to retain the moisture in the substrate. Clear containers work well because you can observe if your gecko has moved dirt around, and sometimes you can lift it to see the eggs in the bottom. I suggest a box 4.5 inches wide, 4 inches deep, and 8 inches long. When you have your container, cut a hole in the top or on the side that is large enough for your gecko to enter. It can be used for up to three females.

You need to place the substrate in it too, and the most used ones are vermiculite, perlite, or sphagnum moss. The depth should be approximately 2 inches. Remember to mist the substrate a little. You do not want the substrate to be super wet, just damp. Moisture also helps the eggs retain water so they do not shrivel up. This is crucial because if they shrivel from lack of moisture, the growing gecko inside will not be able to survive. This box can also double as a humid hide, but access to it typically stimulates egg laying if you think your gecko is ovulating. Once you see your female entering the egg-laying box, please do not check the box for a few hours, or you may disturb and stress her.

When you notice that the eggs have been laid, remove them extremely carefully, as they must remain in their original position/orientation from the time of laying to hatching. Gently place them in the incubator that you prepared.

Incubation

The incubation period can be an anxious time for breeders, particularly beginners. It can be comforting to remind yourself that all you need to monitor and control are temperature and moisture, as both must be right to keep the embryos healthy and growing. It is important to check the humidity/moisture levels and to expose the eggs to fresh air every few days.

If you notice the substrate appears dry or you notice dents in the eggs, you need to provide moisture. Do not spray the eggs but rather drip water at the corners of the container, and it will spread gradually through the substrate. The eggs will recover once the moisture levels are restored.

The other issue to watch for is any sign of bacterial or mold growth on an egg. This is a sure sign the embryo inside has died. Remove the egg immediately before the other egg or eggs become infected.

Chapter 11: Breeding

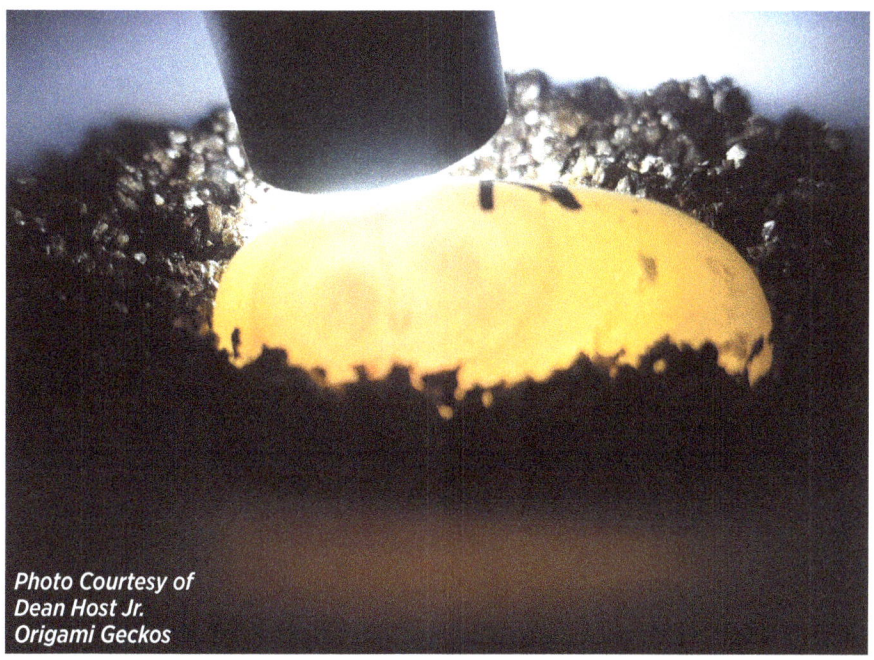
Photo Courtesy of Dean Host Jr. Origami Geckos

In addition to your care and vigilance, there are items of equipment you will need and things that must be done – or not done – to keep the eggs and the developing embryos safe and healthy so you get healthy baby geckos!

Incubators

Once the eggs are laid, you must incubate them, which requires an incubator. There are much higher chances of egg survival using an incubator than just an egg-laying box. Adults can accidentally damage the eggs or eat the hatchlings, so removing the eggs from the parent is safer for the baby. It is also better because incubation requires steady temperatures, and by using an incubator, you can control this.

Moving the eggs

Move them to the incubation box from the egg-laying box. The substrate must be deep enough for the eggs to stay halfway submerged, and it must be slightly damp to keep the eggs hydrated. Place the eggs in the incubation container spaced out from one another by about one inch. Make sure the lid has air holes at the top!

Do not rotate or shake the eggs as you move them around during incubation. They must maintain the same position, so sometimes it can be helpful to mark the eggs very carefully and gently with a marker so you know which side faces up when you first see them in the egg-laying box. You must always place them with the same side facing up. Turning them over or upside down can cause the embryo to drown.

Viable eggs

It is common for a female leopard gecko to lay eggs that are not viable or will not hatch, especially if it is her first-time breeding. If you include children in the breeding process, ensure they understand the process's truths by helping them to understand that there are not always babies inside eggs.

There is an easy way to identify viable and nonviable eggs. At about three days after hatching, fertile or viable eggs are slightly pinkish in color. Infertile eggs will remain soft; the fertilized eggs will become firmer, and the outer coating or "shell" will have a leathery texture.

Temperature-dependent sex determination

One of the surprising and fascinating things about the eggs is that their temperature determines the sex of the leopard gecko that will hatch from it!

When the egg incubation temperature is around 80°F, the hatchlings will mostly be females. If the temperature rises to about 90°F, they will be predominantly males. However, there is a median range where you get a mix of males and females, typically in the mid-80°F range, where 87°F gives a relatively equal ratio of males to females.

It is believed by some that after 21 days, the sex is set and no longer affected by temperature. If the temperatures drop below 74°F, that can be lethal as the embryos cannot survive cold.

Sex	Temperature range
Females	80 to 82°F
Fairly Equal Mix of Male and Female	85 to 87°F
Males	88 to 90°F

Temperature also impacts incubation duration. The incubation period range is six to 10 weeks. If the temperature is higher, they tend to hatch faster.

You will be greeted with an adorable baby leopard gecko when they are ready. The process is truly amazing and a joy to be part of!

Hatching

After 35 to 89 days, the babies will hatch. The temperature in the box or incubator affects which end of the time scale hatching takes place. Droplets of moisture begin to form on the outside of the eggs, and they begin to shrink, so do not panic if it looks as though the eggs are collapsing.

Geckos, like many other species, have an "egg tooth" at the end of their snouts that they use to break through the eggshell. This tooth is calcareous and falls off a day or two after hatching because it has done its job and is no longer needed. These sweet reptiles hatch quietly and relatively quickly, so getting to witness this event is a rare privilege and joy! It is more likely that you will check on the eggs and find they have been replaced by adorable hatchlings.

Hatchlings

Once your baby geckos hatch, keeping them away from adults is important because they may eat the young. When they hatch, they will still have their egg yolk. This is how they will initially feed. They are usually only ready for their first meal after their first shed. This can occur within the first 24 hours and certainly in the first week; after that, they will be ready to hunt small insects. Small mealworms or juvenile crickets are popular choices as feed for these very young hatchlings. Some owners suggest daily feeding, and others believe every other day is preferable. Either way, it is important not to feed them more than five or six days a week, as their tiny digestive systems can become overwhelmed, and this can lead to health problems.

Some breeders suggest that you move the babies into separate containers so that you can monitor an individual's feeding, behavior, and health. However, this is only necessary or feasible if you have large numbers of hatchlings and a lot of equipment and space.

When feeding, it may sometimes be necessary to separate your hatchlings from one another so no one gets bitten by accident while they are still developing their hunting skills. However, they may be housed together or in sibling pairs if they have enough space and are well-fed. As they grow and begin the stages of maturity, they should be housed separately. Some owners suggest well-ventilated plastic boxes that are 12 inches by six inches by 4 inches in size with a paper towel substrate and a very shallow water tray for each hatchling until they reach a length of about 7 inches.

Hatchlings are typically anxious and are not used to humans yet. As a result, they can be snappy. They are also fragile, so avoid handling them until they are older and more robust.

Chapter 11: Breeding

Summary list of items needed for breeding Leopard Geckos

To breed leopard geckos and maximize your chances of success, you will need the following items:

- A male gecko and a female gecko (or several females) that are of the proper age/weight for breeding and in optimal health.
- An egg box for the female to lay her eggs in:
  - A plastic container that is 4.5 inches wide, four inches deep, and eight inches long (for one to three females).
  - Eco Earth substrate or peat moss that has been dampened.
- Spray bottle.
- Egg incubator box:
  - Plastic container with holes in the lid with enough room for eggs to be about one inch apart.
  - Vermiculite or other substrate that has been lightly misted and is deep enough for an egg to be half submerged.
  - A thermometer to check temperatures inside the box.
- Large tank for hatchlings to be separated from adults
- Lots of patience! It is common for this to take a few tries.

While this does indeed represent a not insignificant financial outlay, several of the items are once-off purchases, such as a thermometer and an incubator, which can be used again.

At-a-Glance Fact Sheet

- Leopard Geckos are easy to breed, but is it really what you want to do, and do you have the time, energy, and money to dedicate to it?
- Breeders must learn all about and understand Leopard Gecko genetics.
- Your breeding stock should ideally be a male and one or two females, all of which are 100% healthy, at least one year old, but preferably 2 to 5 years old, or weigh a minimum of 35 grams.
- Prepare your breeding stock by boosting their health with extra food and ensuring they get all the supplements they need.
- You can increase your chances of successful mating by having more than one female but start with only one or two females while you learn the ropes.
- Females lay one or two eggs per clutch or batch of eggs and may lay up to 16 eggs per breeding season.
- Prepare the necessary equipment: a nesting or laying box with a moist substrate in it, an incubator, housing for the hatchlings, and large quantities of suitable feeder insects.
- Eggs are usually laid approximately 21 to 28 days after mating.
- It is common for females to lose their appetite during mating season. Monitor them and provide ample food to replenish the fat stored in their tails when their appetite returns.
- When eggs emerge, they are still soft and take a while to develop their protective shell.
- Pregnant females will begin putting on weight, and you may be able to see the shape of the eggs through her skin.
- Laying signs to look out for in your female are restlessness, digging, and further appetite loss.
- For a nesting site or laying box, you will need a suitable container (4.5 inches wide, 4 inches deep, and 8 inches long) with a lid and a hole cut into the side or top that your gecko can use as an entrance.

At-a-Glance Fact Sheet ...Continued

- Once you see your female entering the egg-laying box, do not disturb her.
- Remove the eggs extremely carefully as they must remain in their original. position/orientation, and place them gently in the incubator.
- There are much higher chances of egg survival using an incubator than just an egg-laying box.
- Temperature during incubation determines the sex of the leopard gecko. With a temperature around 80°F, the hatchlings will mostly be females. If the temperature rises to about 90°F, they will be predominantly males. At a median range, there will be a mix of males and females.
- Temperature also impacts incubation duration. The higher the temperature, the shorter the incubation period.
- The "egg tooth" at the end of the hatchling's snout is used to break through the eggshell. This 'tooth' breaks off after a day or two.
- When they hatch, they will still have their egg yolk, which they feed on at first. They are usually only ready for their first meal after their first shed, which they will eat.
- Small mealworms or juvenile crickets are popular choices as feed for these very young hatchlings.
- Some owners suggest well-ventilated plastic boxes that are 12 inches by 6 inches by 4 inches in size with a paper towel substrate and a very shallow water tray for each hatchling until they reach a length of about 7 inches.
- Hatchlings are fragile and typically anxious and can be snappy. It is advisable to avoid handling them until they are older and more robust.

CHAPTER 12

Other Geckos

While Leopard Geckos are a great choice for beginner reptile owners for all the reasons we have looked at, they are not your only option for great reptilian pets. There are other geckos and reptiles that are popular choices that you could consider.

Other Geckos and Reptilian Pets

If you want to expand your knowledge on different species of geckos, there are many options for eyelid geckos, which are related to Leopard Geckos.

Crested Gecko

Let us start with other geckos and lizards:

African Fat-Tailed Geckos	Chinese Cave Geckos	Banded Geckos
African fat-tailed geckos are from desert regions in West Africa. They are ground lizards and make good pets because they do well in captivity and have a high tolerance for being handled.	Chinese cave geckos are found in China, Vietnam, and Japan. Their habitat is rocky areas with caves near a rainforest. They are ground-dwelling, small, and tolerant of handling.	Banded geckos are ground-dwelling geckos that live in the southwest US, Mexico, and Central America. They are intermediate-level pets as they do not do great with lots of handling. They are also sensitive to husbandry mistakes.

Crested geckos

Many gecko enthusiasts also enjoy the company of **crested geckos,** in part because they, like leopard geckos, are low maintenance. This makes them ideal for beginner reptile owners and older children. They do not need special lighting or care if room temperatures are average and stable. Crested geckos are also easy to handle. They are gentle but hardy animals, and they are adorable.

In the wild, they live in a very different environment than leopard geckos; they like it moist and humid. They have special grips on their feet that allow them to climb glass, and they often leap to the closest surface when being held (to your hand, couch, etc.).

Bearded dragons

Bearded dragons are not geckos, but they are trendy reptilian pets. They are docile and friendly toward humans. They are easy to care for but require high temperatures and UVB lighting in captivity. They are also much bigger lizards than geckos if you want to acquire a larger reptile. They are omnivores and are very easy to handle.

Bearded dragons

Blue-tongued skinks

Blue-tongued skinks are larger than geckos and bearded dragons. They are ground-dwelling and found in Australia and Indonesia. They enjoy burrowing and have voracious appetites for many different prey items, like insects, rodents, snails, and grasshoppers, as well as fruits and vegetables. Blue-tongued skinks have mighty jaws, as they often snack on snails in the wild, shells and all! They require more experience with handling reptiles and should be considered a more advanced pet that is not ideal for beginners.

Chapter 12: Other Geckos

Blue-tongued skinks

But maybe you want something other than – or in addition to – lizards. Here are a few other popular options:

Colubrids

Colubrids like corn snakes, milk snakes, and hognose snakes are great if you are interested in snakes. They are native to many different areas but are relatively cold tolerant during the proper brumation periods, and they are typically docile and appealing as pets. They do require rodent feeding, though frozen-thawed food is preferred for your pet's safety.

Colubrids

Ball pythons

Ball pythons are African snakes that spend much time curled up in tight places in the wild. They are relatively shy but also inquisitive when they trust their human. Their shy behavior is exhibited by curling their bodies into a ball, hence their name. These snakes get much thicker than colubrids but are very popular among reptile keepers. They are desired for the different morphs available through specific breeding.

Ball pythons

Boa constrictors

If you want something larger than a ball python, **boa constrictors** are very docile and handleable. However, they are extremely powerful and should only be considered a suitable option for those with advanced experience. They can weigh over 25 pounds and reach 8 to 10 feet long! Serious commitment is necessary, as they require a lot of space and must be fed big food items like large rats, guinea pigs, or small rabbits.

Boa constrictors

This is certainly not an exhaustive list. If you are interested in owning a reptile but feel unsure about what kind to choose, talk to reptile owners on a forum or visit a specialist reptile store and speak to a staff member about the possibilities.

Selecting a pet is a big and important decision, so you want to get it right and not rush into it!

www.ingramcontent.com/pod-product-compliance
Lightning Source LLC
LaVergne TN
LVHW050131080526
838202LV00061B/6463